LITTLE ANGELS

FOR OUR OWN LITTLE ANGELS – LILY, JACK, EVIE,
TOM AND TEDDY

This book is published to accompany the television series *Little Angels*, first
broadcast on BBC3 in 2003.
Those who worked on the TV series are acknowledged on page 156.

Published by BBC Worldwide Learning, BBC Worldwide Limited,
Woodlands, 80 Wood Lane, London W12 0TT

First published 2005. Copyright © Tanya Byron and Sacha Baveystock
The moral right of the authors has been asserted.

ISBN: 0 563 51941 X

Commissioning Editor: Emma Shackleton
Project Editor: Patricia Burgess
Designer: Annette Peppis
Indexer: Margaret Cornell
Production Controller: Man Fai Lau

Set in Frutiger and Scala
Printed and bound in Great Britain by CPI Bath

LITTLE ANGELS

Dr Tanya Byron & Sacha Baveystock

BBC BOOKS

Contents

chapter one

Whose problem?

'SHE WON'T DO A THING I SAY.' 'IT DOESN'T MATTER HOW MANY TIMES I TELL HIM, he doesn't listen.' 'I'm at my wit's end and beginning to despair.' So ran the stories from the hundreds of parents who rang *Little Angels* asking for help with their children.

You might be reading this because you too are having trouble managing your kids. You may not know what you're doing wrong, but feel you can't cope. You may feel defeated or exhausted. You may even be wondering whether your child needs professional help.

If so, you're in a similar position to many of the families who were keen to take part in the television series. They were the ones who bravely decided to take a leap of faith and confront their problems in the full glare of television publicity. For all of them *Little Angels* was an opportunity to get professional advice on their problems and gain a whole new perspective on where they might be going wrong.

Many had already done the rounds of child experts, read all the books they could lay their hands on, and talked to friends and relatives. They felt, like many people who try to take advice from books or follow tips from others, 'I've tried that and it doesn't work'. But perhaps the key message that they had to take on board when they signed up for the programme was that taking part in *Little Angels* would not be a quick fix either. Just as the process of filming can sometimes be long and arduous, so trying to make changes with your children can take time and effort. Rushing at a problem without thought or planning can only end in failure.

So if at this point your instinct is to go straight to the chapter that deals with your particular problem – don't. Of course you want to start sorting the problem *now*, but it's important to begin with this chapter. The most vital things you need to understand are what your problem is, and whose it is. Many of our *Little Angels* families contacted us for help with a list of problems, only to discover after thinking and talking about it that their view of the problems had drastically changed.

Your very own *Little Angels* programme

Every family who took part in *Little Angels* had to agree to potentially very revealing 'warts and all' filming in their homes over an initial period of two weeks. With their permission, fixed cameras with motion sensors were mounted in their main living spaces to film the family behaving in their usual way. This material was then edited together to make a 'behaviour tape', which one of the series experts – Dr Tanya Byron, Rachel Morris or Dr Stephen Briers – would view and then show to the family.

Right from the beginning the production team would always tell the family, 'Don't change a thing. Act entirely as you always do.' Many of the participants found this a daunting prospect, but it was important for us to get a realistic insight into what was going on within the family. Although some parents tried to moderate their behaviour for the cameras, few were able to keep it up for long, and we were able to experience in a very real way what it was like to be a member of that family.

For the families it was like having a mirror held up to themselves, where they could see how their own behaviour and reactions to their child were part of the problem. Suddenly they were able to see how they were often locked in patterns of behaviour of which they had previously been unaware. For many, watching a tape of themselves was a moment of truth, when suddenly they could see how their *own* behaviour was affecting that of their child. Typical was the moment when Brian Christie realized how much he was shouting at his son Matthew, and when Vicki Wells saw that her constant nagging was actually making her son Oliver behave worse.

So we want you to imagine that you've got those cameras watching you too. Adopting a careful, step-by-step approach, we're going to help you create your own imaginary behaviour tape and thus define your problem. With luck, you'll reach your moment of truth along the way.

What's the problem?

Of course, you can't really mount cameras in your own home. Instead, we suggest you keep a very simple (and private) diary that 'observes' for you. It will help you to recognize patterns of behaviour and triggers to the problem. Most importantly, it will help you look at how you respond to your children when they are behaving in a way you don't like.

You need to be as honest and realistic in your record-keeping as if there really were cameras present. You might be groaning inwardly at the horror of having to put up with more difficult behaviour, but it's important to realize that there is no way you will be able to change things if you don't have this information to hand. Don't try to rush into changing things. Allow the problem to continue for at least a week while you record all examples of it.

Before you can think about changing behaviour you need to be clear about what it is you want to change. You may be able to describe broadly what the problem is, for example, 'My daughter won't sleep' or 'Our son behaves aggressively', but that still isn't enough to enable you to start problem-solving. For instance, does 'won't sleep' mean 'won't go to sleep in her bed', or 'won't sleep through the night in her bed', or 'will stay in her bed, but wakes and calls out 20 times during the night'? All are real sleep problems, but each is different, and differing approaches are needed to change them. You therefore need to be as specific as you can in understanding the details of your problem.

What is normal?

Of the vast numbers of families who contacted the programme, the overwhelming majority were asking for help with behaviour, particularly tantrums and aggression. The other most common problems we've seen on *Little Angels* have been fighting, defiance, sleep problems, disobedience, feeding, toilet behaviour and emotional problems, particularly anxiety and low self-esteem.

But to what extent are these 'bad' behaviour? Many parents don't know what to expect of their children. Your first step is to think about whether what you see as the problem actually is a problem. Do you see other children of the same age behaving like this? Or is it more to do with your own uncertainties as a parent? Do you actually know what behaviour is acceptable at what age?

For example, most children are going to whinge, whine and not want to do what they're asked. Most siblings fight, hit, scream and hurl accusations. Many toddlers are strong-willed and can have tantrums several times a day. It's therefore useful to consider whether children's behaviour at different ages is normal. A two-year-old throwing himself on to the floor and having a tantrum is common behaviour for that age group, but it isn't normal for a six-year-old. A one-year-old having problems with settling herself off to sleep is more common than a child of four who still needs to sleep in your bed.

It's also important to remember that children come with their own personalities, which obviously affect their behaviour. Take a look at your own family and you will see how siblings are all very different people. What we are like depends on our genes and the environment in which we live. Add to that gender differences, birth order and early life experiences and you begin to see how each one of us is unique.

Although we are offering you techniques for managing child behaviour, it's also important to relax about your 'problem child' and begin to acknowledge that at least some of his behaviour is part of who he is. It's worth reminding yourself that the problems you are so concerned about do not make your child abnormal – and there are often many other parents in the same boat.

Starting your diary

On page 12 is an example of a simple diary that you can use to monitor the problem behaviour. It is easy to follow, and should be kept for a minimum of one week. The example below shows how you would monitor problems such as tantrums and aggression.

The first rule of keeping a diary is to make sure that you record each and every event as soon after it happened as possible, otherwise you'll forget it. This must be an accurate record of the problem behaviour, not just in terms of what goes on, but also how often and when. Keep the diary in an exercise book so that you can carry with you when you go out and make entries in it at any time.

It's worth continuing to keep your diary once you start to make changes, as it will help you chart how things are changing – for example, whether a certain behaviour is happening less often during a single day. Over time this will help you to look back and see how change is really happening.

To begin, take a standard exercise book, turn it sideways and draw up a chart across the width of the page (as shown below). Give yourself most room for columns A, B and C.

WHAT TO WRITE ON YOUR CHART

Day/date/ time	A Where you are & what's happening	B Your child's behaviour	C Your response	Outcome
Note whether the problems occur at a particular time of day, and if so, what might be triggering them.	'A' stands for antecedents, the psychologists' term for triggers.	'B' stands for behaviour. Describe exactly what your child does.	'C' stands for consequence. Note how you are reacting.	Note how your reaction is affecting the behaviour.

This might sound like a lot of hard work. But remember, knowledge is power, and you need to do this in the short term to find long-term answers. This information can only increase your range of potential solutions.

SAMPLE BEHAVIOUR DIARY

(kept by Sam Norris, mother of three-year-old Katie)

Day/ date/ time	A Where you are & what's happening	B Describe your child's behaviour	C Describe your response	Outcome
Mon 12th 9.30 a.m.	In car, going shopping.	Screaming and hitting sister.	Yelled to stop and tried to smack.	All yelling at each other – very stressed when got to shops.
Mon 12th 10.30 a.m.	At home, trying to unpack shopping.	Wants a lolly and screaming and trying to bite me when I say no.	1. Tried to explain that it was too early for a lolly. 2. After she bit me I shouted and bit her back to show her it hurt.	Tantrum on the floor, kicking out at me.
Mon 12th 11.30 a.m.	In lounge, drinking tea.	Bit and hit her sister, who wouldn't share a toy.	Shouted and pulled her away and smacked her.	Massive tantrum, crying and hitting me.

Understanding your diary

Now go through the A, B, C headings to work out what is happening.

Time of day: Mornings seem like a stressful time. Everyone is wound up and stress levels are high. Remember, if you feel stressed and out of control, so will your child.

A – Antecedents (triggers): Katie kicks off when Sam is doing something that doesn't involve her, such as unpacking the shopping. Is this the way she is learning to get her mother's attention? She does not understand that when Sam says no she means it. If Katie is not getting any attention from Sam when she is behaving well, she will learn to misbehave in order for her to notice.

B – Behaviour: Katie is physically and verbally aggressive, screaming, hitting, kicking, biting and throwing herself on the floor. She is having temper tantrums and seems to have learnt how her challenging behaviour can control others.

C – Consequence: Sam's behaviour mirrors Katie's. She also screams, hits and bites. If you don't want your child to behave aggressively, do not use aggressive responses; it will give children a confusing message about what is acceptable. Also, Sam tries to reason with a frustrated three-year-old about not having a lolly in the morning. Three-year-olds don't have the intellectual capacity to understand and process a reasoned argument about why they can't have what they want.

Outcome: Sam's responses and behaviour do two things – they make the problem behaviour go on for longer, and make it more likely to be repeated. Sam's behaviour is therefore part of the problem.

So who needs to change?

This is the crucial question you need to ask yourself. Who are we changing? Sam's diary clearly shows that Katie needs to stop her behaviour, as it is aggressive and makes everyone, including herself, feel unhappy. If it carries on into her school years, it could affect her relationships with other children, and possibly lead to social and educational problems. However, Sam's behaviour shows that she acts in a very similar manner to her three-year-old. You have to ask: who is the adult here?

If you're immediately thinking, 'So it's all my fault,' it's important to put this into perspective. First, none of us is perfect, and if we were, our children would grow up with an odd view of the world. Children have to see us make mistakes in order to learn vital living skills. Second, if we begin to accept that we, rather than our child, are the problem, it makes life easier, as all we need to do is change our own behaviour and, with luck, our child's will too as a result. Third, as soon as we can stop viewing our child as The Problem, the quicker she will stop being one.

If you are finding it hard to accept that you could be the problem, and you haven't gathered any evidence from your diary yet, just remember that children learn from us and we shape their behaviour. If a child is given a sweet every time he has a tantrum, he will quickly learn that the best way to get a sweet is to have a tantrum. How the behaviour is treated has a huge bearing on whether that behaviour continues or not.

Dee Georgiou couldn't bear it when his daughter Nicola had a tantrum. He wanted the noise to stop, so he tried to grab hold of her, cuddle her, and even offered her treats. In asking her, 'Shall I buy you anything you want?' he gave Nicola a very confusing message, suggesting that her tantrum would be rewarded. As a loving dad, he meant well, but what he failed to see was how he was reinforcing the behaviour he didn't want by treating it this way.

But you might then ask how a more negative reaction to a pattern of behaviour could still make that behaviour happen again and again. If Brian was shouting at Matthew, why did his child keep on doing what he was being asked not to? This is when you need to consider your behaviour at other times. How do you behave when your child is not being a problem? Your child will respond to whatever attention she gets the most of, so if you're shouting and nagging, you'll see *more* of the behaviour you're shouting and nagging at. While you are keeping your diary, it's worth noting how often you praise your child – something Brian realized he wasn't doing as often as he might.

What are you doing?

Given our busy lives, we probably all spend more time telling our kids off than praising them. This isn't because we want to be nasty to them. But at the times when they're quiet and settled, we probably leave them be while we get on with things that need to be done. Meanwhile, as soon as the problems start, we race in and start shouting. Our reaction to the behaviour has a big influence on whether it keeps happening.

Consider the following two scenarios:

1 Jo Barton is downstairs getting on with chores, while three-year-old Elliot and five-year-old Luke are playing in their bedroom.

2 Elliot throws a block at his brother's head, and before long a major fight has broken out. Within seconds, Jo is up in the bedroom intervening, drying tears and giving cuddles.

Children love attention and parents are their main source of attention. So which of the two scenarios is likely to happen most often? It's number two of course.

At this point you may be thinking of all the times when you have made an effort to give more praise and cuddles, yet the children have still been as much of a pain. Unfortunately, changing behaviour isn't that simple. If, over time, you have given most attention to your children's problem behaviour, you will need to work at consciously giving more of your attention to their lovely behaviour. At the same time, you will have to help them unlearn what you have taught them, and that's going to take effort, patience and consistency on your part.

What does the behaviour mean?

Once you have accepted that in order to change your child's behaviour you may have to change your own, you need to consider what the behaviour itself means. This is important, as sometimes our interpretation of the behaviour can make us react in a way that makes the problem worse.

A common mistake among the parents we met on *Little Angels* was to imagine that their children had far greater reasoning skills than was possible for their age. The part of the brain that enables us to manage our behaviour and act sensibly and rationally is the frontal lobes. This area is still developing in the early years, and isn't fully functioning in an adult sense. Having lengthy conversations with your young children about the rights and wrongs of their behaviour will get you nowhere, except give them loads of attention and hence strengthen the behaviour you want rid of. (See Developmental Checklist, page 18.)

'I just feel he's trying to belittle me, so he's in control,' Lisa Williams said of her four-year-old son Kieran. She didn't realize that four-year-olds lack the sophisticated powers of reasoning to think through the emotional impact of their behaviour on another person. Kieran was simply arguing back with her because she was giving him loads of attention when arguing with him.

It is vital to recognize that your responses to your child's behaviour may reflect more what you think is going on than what your child is actually feeling. Rage might be interpreted by worried parents as huge emotional pain, and tantrums as deep-rooted insecurity.

Emily Soilleux, for example, was constantly having tantrums that left her parents exhausted. Her mother Jane was wracked with guilt at Emily's tears whenever she wanted to leave the house without her. But Jane didn't realize that Emily wasn't voicing emotional torment: she was just annoyed, and her way of expressing that at three years of age was simply to scream and throw herself on the floor. Jane wasn't able to see that the minute she had gone, Emily's tears promptly stopped. Once Jane was able to recognize that she was witnessing rage rather than deep trauma, she was able to distance herself far more easily from the tantrums and manage them more effectively.

If you interpret your child's behaviour from an adult perspective, you will mismanage the behaviour, give it too much attention and increase your problems. Jo Barton wouldn't let Luke have first choice of ice cream for pudding because he hadn't finished his lunch, so Luke slid under the table in a sulk. But rather than just ignore him until he stopped sulking, the whole family got caught up in Luke's sulk. Eventually both parents were trying to coax him out with various temptations, including more ice creams, but he couldn't actually manage this logically, and simply became grumpier. His parents' response reinforced the grumpy behaviour: he's getting attention for it, so he does it more. Meanwhile, his brother Elliot, who had eaten his meal and behaved well, got his ice cream and left the table, getting no attention for his good behaviour. If Jo hadn't been drawn into Luke's sulk and 'hurt feelings', it's more likely that the sulk would have quickly blown over.

What else is happening?

When we are feeling stressed and anxious by our children's behaviour, we can become very fixed in our thinking. This means that rather than think about what our child is doing and why she is doing it, we rush in headlong with a reaction that may actually increase that particular behaviour.

Three-year-old Ella Price dominated the life of her family with her biting and tantrums, but her parents Nigel and Bianca hadn't considered what might have been the cause of her behaviour. They just saw her as a difficult child. The family behaviour tapes revealed that Ella and her two brothers aged seven and five routinely stayed up until 10.30 p.m., watching videos in their room. Nigel and Bianca weren't neglectful parents; they had simply slipped into a bad routine. They were unable to objectively link Ella's difficult behaviour to her lack of sleep. By looking at the bigger picture, they were able to appreciate that Ella wasn't a monster – just sleep-deprived.

Jay Cooper's aggression towards his brother Owen was terrifying his mother Kathy. She felt he was capable of extreme violence, so avoided contact with him. But by being helped to think about the bigger picture, Kathy was able to recognize that Jay was acting out violence he had witnessed as a young child. Kathy's physical fear of Jay was in fact increasing his anxiety, making it hard for him to distinguish between appropriate and inappropriate types of physical contact. This was then escalating the problem.

What's with you?

Jay's past experiences clearly played a big part in his behaviour problems. When Tanya, Rachel or Stephen started working with the families on the programme, among the first questions they asked were, 'Can you pinpoint when the behaviour started? Was there anything else going on at the time?' Parents would often have a moment of truth as they realized that they could link the behaviour back to a particular point of stress or difficulty in their own lives. Children are incredibly good at picking up the vibes in their family, so it's worth thinking about

DEVELOPMENTAL CHECKLIST

Check below to see what to expect from children of different ages.

Age	Behaviour
1 year	Early walking; begins playing; calm and friendly if feels safe; enjoys building and makes lines on paper.
2 years	Temper tantrums; learns to use the word 'no'; may go through phase of hitting and biting; says words, phrases and simple sentences; likes to look at books; short attention span.
3 years	Plays side by side; takes turns; knows own gender; helpful, but may occasionally have tantrum or frustrated rage. Short sentences; answers questions; wants to understand the environment.
4 years	Increasingly independent behaviour, e.g. dressing, drawing, cutting out. Can manipulate a situation if given the opportunity.
5 years	Can dress self; establishing reading and writing with confidence; conversational; cooperative play; 'special' friends; enjoys responsibility.
6–9 years	Cooperates with other children; likes rules to be observed; looking for approval and can be self-critical; aware of peer issues; loyal to friends; pushing boundaries at times.

Emotions	Sleep	Eating/Toilet
Building trust and bonding; loves play and praise; curious, exploring; separation anxiety; fear of strangers.	Approx. 11$\frac{1}{2}$–12 hours per night, plus 1–3 hours of naps.	Needs to be fed; exploring tastes and textures; regular mealtime pattern, plus snacks. In nappies.
Self-centred; shows frustration and rage; more impulsive; loves play and praise; increasing independence.	Approx. 11–11$\frac{1}{2}$ hours per night; 1–1$\frac{1}{2}$-hour nap.	Experiments with self-feeding. Beginning to establish bowel and bladder control.
More easygoing attitude; more flexible to change; more secure; greater personal identity; becoming adventurous; loves play and praise.	11 hours per night; 1-hour nap.	Self-feeding, with a good range of foods in diet; if not, could become 'faddy'. Dry by day; may also be dry by night.
Strong sense of self; can be defiant; needs freedom with boundaries; developing moral sense of right and wrong.	11$\frac{1}{2}$ hours per night; no naps.	Successful self-feeding; knows food likes and dislikes; 'faddy' if has been given control of food choices. Dry by day, and mostly at night.
Self-confident; clear sense of right and wrong; can assess own behaviour; enjoys being responsible; likes rules and to know where he/she stands.	11 hours	Full range of foods; fully self-feeding; can make food choices.
Increasing confidence, but can have mood swings; sensitive and can be self-critical; needs encouragement and praise or can become easily discouraged; life and death questions; questions about the body.	10–11 hours	As above.

some of the problems you may have been facing when they started acting up. Have you been depressed or anxious? Have you been facing divorce, job loss, bereavement? All these things will have an impact on your child.

Now you're ready to start your diary. Remember, be consistent, stick with it – and good luck!

Diary checklist

Your diary could help you to think more broadly about what is causing the problem behaviour. As you mull over what you have recorded, ask yourself the following questions:

- ○ Is there a most difficult time of day?
- ○ Are there particular triggers to the problem behaviour?
- ○ Is the behaviour something my child has seen/experienced/copied?
- ○ Is my child behaving like this because he is tired/hungry/frightened?
- ○ What am I doing to make the behaviour worse?
- ○ What am I doing to keep the behaviour going?
- ○ Is anything else happening in my life that may be affecting my child?

POINTS TO REMEMBER

○ All children will exhibit behaviour problems at some time: it is part of development and provides them with an opportunity to learn self-management and social skills. We must be realistic about what constitutes a 'behaviour problem' by thinking about what is appropriate for the child's age and stage of development.

○ As parents, we exert the most powerful influence over our children's learning and behaviour. Our responses to their behaviour have a huge and lasting impact on whether the behaviour continues or not.

○ In our busy lives we tend to give our children more attention if they are behaving in a way that we don't like than if they are behaving well, when we often leave them to get on with it.

○ For a child, being shouted at and told off is still attention, particularly if we don't give him enough positive attention at other times. Children quickly learn that behaving in a certain way will get attention.

○ Before we can change a problem behaviour we have to understand it. A minimum of a week must be spent monitoring the problem behaviour before deciding on strategies for change.

○ Diaries and reflection can show that the most important changes need to come from us as parents. Our responses to our child's behaviour can both increase and encourage that behaviour.

○ Don't over-analyse the meaning of the behaviour. Many parents misinterpret rage as long-term emotional trauma, and in doing so reinforce the tantrum with too much attention.

○ Your child's behaviour may be a symptom of a bigger underlying problem. For example, tantrums may reflect sleep deprivation. Be clear as to which problem needs to be dealt with first.

○ Young children do not have the capacity to fully understand discussions about behaviour. Long chats and over-negotiation will only fuel the behaviour by giving it lots of attention, while the children are learning nothing more than how to get themselves noticed.

○ In order to change our child's problem behaviour, we first have to change our own.

chapter two

You can change

'I WAS AFRAID THAT TANYA WAS GOING TO TELL ME I WAS A BAD MOTHER,' SAID Alev Huseyin of her first visit from *Little Angels*. Like many of those who participated in the series, she and her husband Somer didn't know quite what to expect of their meeting with a clinical psychologist. But Alev's fears suggested that she knew in her heart where the root of the problem might lie.

In fact, Alev was far from a bad mother. But it quickly became apparent that she and Somer had got locked into a pattern of negative beliefs about their children. It was a relief for them to realize that there was nothing wrong with the children and that the real business of change had to start with themselves. For many of the other parents who took part in the series, actually taking ownership of the problem and realizing that it was more about them than their child was almost a liberation.

But suddenly shifting perspective on whose problem you are dealing with is no easy task. You might feel like we're asking you to achieve the impossible. Being positive and confident that you can change can seem simply beyond you.

So if you are now thinking and feeling that you too are a 'bad parent', this is another very important chapter for you to read before you rush on to specific problem-solving. The process begins and ends with you, so it's vital that you feel good about yourself and what you're trying to achieve. It's important that you understand how your attitudes towards yourself as a parent and to your child can affect the success of any changes you try to make.

The voice in your ear

A key part of every *Little Angels* programme focused on coaching, which Tanya, Stephen or Rachel would provide via an earpiece (known to the team as an 'earbug') directly connected to the parent's ear. This way the expert could talk the parent through potentially challenging situations, from shopping to mealtimes, or sometimes just teach parents how to interact or play more happily with their child.

Obviously, you don't have your very own expert in your ear, so it's important to develop your own inner voice, which will speak to you in positive and encouraging ways. To achieve this you'll first need to explore any negative beliefs that you may have, which could thwart the success of your attempts to change. We hope to enable you to adopt a more positive approach by challenging those beliefs and the more undermining thoughts that you may have when stressed by your child's behaviour.

They're in control

This is how Alev Huseyin described her family: 'We are not the parents: I feel that we have no control over this house.' When Alev first contacted the programme her children Ayla and Esin, aged three and 18 months, were very difficult to manage. Ayla in particular could be aggressive and defiant, and had long, violent temper tantrums. She had also never fallen asleep or slept through the night in her own bed. Alev, who was eight months pregnant with her third child, was exhausted, and the marriage was under severe stress as a result of the difficulties she and Somer were having with their children.

On the surface what Alev said about having no control appeared to be true. But the reality was that until she and Somer could shift their negative belief that the children in their household held the power, the children would continue to dominate them. If you look at your children and think that they, rather than you, have the control, this reflects a belief about yourself that suggests you will not be able to change either your own behaviour or your children's.

Tamara Carrera is a single mother to four-year-old Keanu. She contacted *Little Angels* for help with his unruly, domineering behaviour, which left her feeling exhausted and unhappy. She felt powerless to control him, and consequently had no confidence in herself as a mother. 'He's got it in his mind that he's the king of the castle and what he says goes,' she told us.

While watching her behaviour tape, Tamara became increasingly distressed as she realized for the first time that her nagging Keanu and arguing with him was contributing to his problems. 'I'm going to make him a negative person just like me. He's not going to be confident,' she said. It was a painful realization, but one that spurred her to challenge her underlying negative belief that she was a hopeless mother who couldn't achieve change.

It was important for Tamara to begin the process of change by addressing her own self-doubts first. She began with small tasks, such as taking Keanu out – something she often avoided because she was so afraid that she wouldn't be able to control him – and enjoying some positive interaction with him.

During an earpiece session in the park, Tamara was able to see how, instead of focusing on all the stuff that drove her mad, praising and playing with Keanu helped her enjoy him in a way she hadn't before. Although initially self-conscious, she noticed how he responded to her as she gave him more positive encouragement. She began to see how constructive and positive play with Keanu improved his behaviour and strengthened the bond between them, more than her shouting at him ever had.

Similarly, Lisa Williams had got herself locked into a negative mindset about her four-year-old son Kieran. She was convinced that he was dominating her in a power play: 'Kieran does rule this house,' she said. 'He'll actually say to me, "I'm the boss". He thrives on winding me up.' What Lisa couldn't see was that she was constantly setting Kieran up to behave badly, and the more she responded to his swearing and arguing, the more he swore and argued. When she said, 'I dread going to town because I know for a fact that he's going to play me up,' her negative belief made it more likely that he really would play her up when they went out.

Lisa had got caught in a negative pattern partly because she was so angry with Kieran's dad, from whom she'd parted when Kieran was one. What she had lost sight of was that her four-year-old son was arguing with her to get her attention because he got no reward for the times when he did behave well. When Lisa began to pay Kieran more positive attention and focus on him in a more engaging way, he began to calm down – and behaved beautifully when she eventually took him into town.

They won't change

Nigel Price was another parent who held a belief about his children that, unless challenged, would undermine any attempt to change their behaviour. Miles, Herbie and Ella, seven, five and three respectively, never went to bed in the evening, and were often awake watching videos in their shared bedroom until 10.30 p.m. This meant that they were all sleep-deprived, which was having a noticeable impact on their behaviour.

It was a shock for Nigel and his partner Bianca to be told that in order to change the behaviour that was frustrating them – the fighting, tantrums and defiance – they'd have to tackle their children's sleep problems first. Both parents looked dumbfounded when it was suggested to them that the children had to be made to go to bed earlier, and Nigel expressed his negative belief very clearly, saying, 'I just don't see how that could happen.'

Both Nigel and Bianca needed some persuasion to shift their negative belief into the positive one: they *will* go to bed. During an earpiece session, Nigel was successfully talked through putting the kids to bed and dealing with their protests (which were not as strong as he had anticipated). But it was only when Nigel, a jazz musician, left for work that evening after successfully getting his children into bed two hours earlier than normal that he realized he could shift his expectations both of his kids and of himself as a parent. Within a few days, all the children were going to bed earlier, and the family began to see a marked improvement in their behaviour. An added bonus was that the oldest child, Miles, began to perform much better at school.

By believing that the children wouldn't sleep, Nigel had in fact set up the whole family to fail. The reason for this is very simple: if you hold strong beliefs about your children and their behaviour, you are more likely to treat them in a way that will make them go on behaving that way. It's called the self-fulfilling prophecy. In other words, what you predict will come true.

The self-fulfilling prophecy

Every family tends to have its labels. 'He's the bright one,' you might say, or 'She's the party girl'. In Jane and Barry Soilleux's family they had a label for three-year-old Emily: 'She's the whinger.' Emily was indeed a whinger, but by labelling her this way Jane and Barry were in fact setting her up to whinge all the more. This is an example of a self-fulfilling prophecy.

It's not unusual for parents to have one of their children marked as the 'naughty one', another example of the self-fulfilling prophecy. Three-year-old Katie Norris's parents, Sam and Tim, had her labelled as a rebel and a tearaway. 'She wears the trousers,' Sam said of Katie, so she did.

On the face of it Katie could be labelled a 'naughty child'. She was having long tantrums, screaming when she didn't get her own way and not sleeping through the night, constantly calling out and waking her two-year-old sister, Amy. Katie also bit and hit her sister and parents. However, it also became very clear that because Sam and Tim had cast Katie in the role of the 'bad one', while Amy was their little angel, they were often inadvertently setting up Katie to behave badly.

When Sam and Tim watched their behaviour tapes they were quickly able to see how they triggered the bad behaviour in Katie – this was their emotional moment of truth. In one clip Katie was playing happily alone on the floor with some cushions for 10 minutes, while Sam and Tim watched TV. Amy muscled in on the game and tried to grab the cushions, and Katie tried to pull her sister away, at which point Sam and Tim looked up. Both immediately started shouting at Katie and threw a cushion at her. Katie rolled away, crying, and was threatened with being sent to her room while her father comforted Amy in a very different tone of voice.

Since Sam and Tim believed that Katie was difficult, they would automatically assume that she was at fault whenever there was a problem. This meant she was always being blamed, and getting attention only when she behaved badly, which of course would increase her bad behaviour, particularly as she was rarely praised by her parents. Sam and Tim were turning their three-year-old daughter into a difficult child by believing that she was one.

I'm scared

It's not just the children that some parents hold negative beliefs about; it's themselves as parents too. Many of those we talked to felt unsure about their parenting capabilities, and lacked confidence in managing their children. In our busy and competitive world it is easy to see why, but it's vital you don't let a lack of confidence act as a block to improving your child's behaviour. When we feel anxious our instinct is to avoid the situation or person making us feel that way. But avoidance actually increases our anxieties, as we have no evidence to challenge our perception that we can't cope.

Sue Angell is a full-time working mother of two children: nine-year-old Bethany from her first marriage and three-year-old Emily from her second marriage to Ivan, who looks after the girls while Sue is at work. Sue and Ivan contacted Little Angels because they were worried about Ivan's relationship with his stepdaughter Bethany, and both had difficulties with tantrum-prone Emily.

Sue was undoubtedly feeling very stressed by the situation. 'I only have to hear that first cry and it sends me to a place of absolute hell,' she said of Emily's tantrums. Instead of trying to deal with them, she would often run away to another room, or break down in tears herself. Sue was particularly scared of Emily screaming while they were out shopping, and it was not unusual for her to end up in tears in the supermarket, feeling anxious about her daughter's loud behaviour and embarrassed by the staring of other shoppers. She would never go out with both girls for fear that 'World War Three' would break out.

Emily had learnt how to get her own way, and by giving in to her Sue and Ivan were showing that she *could* be in control. But as they avoided going out for fear of how Emily might behave, they actually increased the problem behaviour. Both girls were frustrated being stuck at home, and were then more likely to misbehave. By not going out, Sue could never experience any fun time with her daughters. Yet this was exactly what she needed to do to start believing that she could manage them, which would in turn increase her confidence as a mother. Sue was trapped in a vicious circle.

Filming with *Little Angels* helped Sue to confront her worst fear. We took her for an earpiece session to the supermarket, where first she had to try to distract Emily from having a tantrum, and then ignore it when the inevitable happened. It was a vital opportunity for Sue to begin managing her automatic negative thoughts about not being able to cope, and she decided to sing 'Que Sera Sera' as a way of distracting herself. Emily continued to have her tantrum, but this time was faced with a mother who was unmoved by her behaviour and not reinforcing it with any attention. Sue even noticed that most passers-by gave her looks of sympathy; those who didn't she just ignored.

At the end of the trip, despite the fact that Emily had screamed her way around the supermarket, Sue was jubilant. 'I expected it, every situation that she thinks will test me to the absolute limit...I was expecting her to behave like that, but I was able to keep my head up and I'm not stressed,' she proclaimed. She had conquered her fear.

The vicious circle

Anxiety comes from negative beliefs. If you believe you are a bad parent, you will feel anxious and stressed when you're with your children. As little barometers of mood, children are very affected by feelings of anxiety; it can make them feel anxious themselves, and they start playing up to get your attention. Also, they will quickly learn to read you, so when they sense you are stressed they'll know how to push your buttons. If, like Sue and Ivan, you eventually give in for a 'quiet life', they'll know how to get what they want.

One way to consider how your anxiety about your children's behaviour affects your ability to parent them is expressed in the following formula:

How we THINK ➤ How we FEEL ➤ How we BEHAVE

Our negative thoughts come out of our negative beliefs. If you go into a situation thinking you will fail, the chances are that you will. The formula above applied to Sue Angell's experience would be:

BELIEF: I can't control my child ➤ THOUGHT when in supermarket: 'I am losing control, I can't cope' ➤ FEELING when in supermarket: anxious, stressed and wanting to leave ➤ BEHAVIOUR: crying/walking out/shouting at child ➤ BELIEF strengthened: 'I definitely can't control my child, I am a bad mother.'

Anxiety is also called the fight or flight syndrome, and is a primitive in-built survival mechanism to help us deal with threat. If you find your children's behaviour threatening and start feeling out of control and anxious, you will either fight them, by shouting or smacking, or withdraw from them, by crying or leaving the situation. Both these responses give your children the message that they are powerful, making it more likely that they will continue to behave in the way that makes you anxious. As Sue found, this then increases your belief that you really are a bad parent and can't cope.

By facing her fear and challenging her beliefs, Sue's thinking became more like this:

BELIEF: I *can* control my child ➤ THOUGHT when in supermarket: 'I am in control, I can cope' ➤ FEELING when in supermarket: confident to ignore child and remain calm ➤ BEHAVIOUR: staying calm and ignoring my child, who is just having a tantrum ➤ BELIEF strengthened: 'I can definitely control my child, I am a good mother.'

Quelling your fear

If you feel anxious and find that you are avoiding certain places because you fear how your child might behave, you are in fact making the problem worse, as neither you nor your child will have any experience of your managing well. The way to counter this is by slowly going into the feared places.

○ Start with short trips. Enter, talking to yourself positively. Do not let the negative thoughts make you run and leave.

○ Distract yourself from your stressed thinking by singing to yourself, or focusing on a relaxing image, or counting backwards in threes from 100. Do anything you can to keep the undermining thoughts at bay so that you can brave it out and show yourself that you can be in control.

○ Always give yourself a chance to succeed by leaving when the behaviour is still going well. This way you'll build up your confidence. It might mean that initially you are in the feared place for only three minutes, but that is three minutes more positive than you ever experienced before. Build up slowly.

○ Most of all, be realistic and don't set yourself the weekly shop for your first outing. See these steps as a series of experiments to prove to yourself that you can master your anxieties, and in doing so begin to believe in yourself as a parent.

It's no fun

As soon as Sue Angell began to master her anxieties and feel more in control, she began to enjoy her relationship with both her children much more. Another *Little Angels* parent, Zora Lunniss, also needed a lot of support to shift her beliefs and feel more positive about herself as a mother.

Zora's identical twin girls Asha and Elodie were three, and she had a son Joe, 13, from a previous relationship. Having really enjoyed Joe as a young child, Zora was confused and upset by the realization that she was not enjoying her twins. She found them demanding and difficult, prone to tantrums, and uncooperative to the point that even trying to get their hair cut resulted in Zora leaving the salon upset and frustrated, without the girls' hair having been cut.

Zora was feeling increasingly unhappy about her and the girls' relationship: 'I absolutely love them to death, but I don't like them a lot of the time, and I feel that they don't like me a lot of the time either,' she admitted. She felt that her days were a series of tasks that had to be got through, and would wake each morning with a sense of dread. In short, it was no fun. 'It's just so tiring and relentless. I must be doing something wrong for them to be like that,' she said.

Zora needed help to recognize how the girls' premature birth, when she had been unable to breastfeed them, had taken its toll on her, leaving her with feelings of anxiety and an overwhelming sense that she hadn't bonded with them. This resulted in her feeling increasingly depressed and isolated, which made the three-way relationship tense and unhappy. 'Because I'm miserable it's making them miserable,' she realized after seeing herself on tape. 'It's kind of what I knew anyway, but seeing it proves it.' It was her moment of truth.

Like Sue Angell, Zora needed help to build a more positive belief system about herself and the girls by putting herself in challenging situations that she could master. The obvious choice was a trip to the hairdresser. Once there, the situation quickly deteriorated because Zora revealed her lack of confidence by letting the girls choose who went first. Sensing her anxiety, they quickly started crying, which in turn increased Zora's feelings of helplessness. It was all spiralling towards another unsuccessful trip.

Zora was told through the earpiece to be authoritative and make it clear to Asha that her hair was going to be cut. At first Asha was upset and struggled, but Zora held her firmly in a body hug and gave her lots of encouragement until she calmed down. When Elodie saw Asha getting so much attention and praise she was soon drawn in and clamouring for her own turn. 'I was very surprised,' Zora admitted. 'I didn't think that was ever going to happen.' Beyond the actual hair-cut, the most important aspect of this experience was that Zora felt a real sense of achievement as a mother. As her confidence began to increase, she felt less afraid of the twins' behaviour and more able to enjoy them. Within weeks, she was feeling much closer to them and having more fun. 'Do I think I'm a good mum? Sometimes,' she concluded. 'But I don't think I'm a bad mother any more.'

Piecing it all together

The story of the Isherwood family highlights how sometimes a series of different beliefs can interact to affect behaviour at every level within the family.

Teresa Isherwood's relationship with her eldest child, Dominic, had never felt good. She and her husband Adam had two other children: three-year-old Cameron and baby Lauren. Teresa and Adam had contacted *Little Angels* because they felt that Dominic had severe behaviour problems, was defiant and difficult to manage. 'He's disrespectful towards me, he's got lots of attitude,' claimed Teresa. 'It would be nice if we could make him so he was nicer towards me.'

From the beginning it was clear that Dominic was a normal, lively six-year-old and did not have severe behaviour problems. In fact, given Teresa's history of depression and that the family had moved house 10 times since he was born, his behaviour seemed remarkably settled. So where was the problem? The problem lay with Adam and Teresa's beliefs about themselves as parents and about their son.

Teresa very much saw Dominic as the 'bad boy' of the family. She found his siblings much easier to manage, and even felt she loved them more than Dominic. 'I always seem to be cross with him; I know it's something inside me that finds it difficult to be close to him,' she confessed. By casting him in the 'bad' role, she was always on the lookout for him to behave badly. It had got to the point that even innocent play-fighting with his brother was perceived as bullying. This in itself was a self-fulfilling prophecy.

Teresa also felt helpless in her parenting of Dominic, and would wait until his father got home from work to tell tales of his bad behaviour. Adam would then have to intervene, leaving Teresa feeling less confident about her own parenting skills, and Adam feeling uncertain that disciplining Dominic was the right approach. Adam was anxious about disagreeing with his wife in front of the children, but they often disagreed about how to deal with Dominic's behaviour, which compounded the problems and built up resentments.

Finally, Teresa could never have fun or enjoy her time with Dominic because she was so afraid that he would misbehave. This meant that despite living two minutes away from a park, she had never gone there with him. In a very moving moment, Teresa wept as she confessed her fear that if she did ask her son to play with her, he might reject her. Her strategy was to avoid the issue altogether.

Teresa and Adam needed help to acknowledge that their negative beliefs about their son were primarily responsible for what they thought was his problem behaviour. But they also had to look at how they felt about themselves. Both of them were shy and rarely went out; they had few friends as a result of having moved so often, and Teresa in particular found it difficult to meet other mothers. As a very sociable and popular child, Dominic was challenging his parents' anxious beliefs about socializing: the more time he spent with his friends, the more Teresa and Adam's anxieties increased, leaving them more convinced that his behaviour was problematic. In an earpiece exercise Teresa was forced to challenge her belief that people would never want to talk to her by striking up a conversation with another mother in a park. It was something she dreaded doing, but was actually able to achieve with ease.

Even more difficult for Teresa and Adam was the realization that these negative beliefs about their son were what united them as a couple. Accepting Dominic for who he was meant that they were forced to recognize the real problems in their marriage. Taking part in the programme meant that they decided to seek marriage counselling. Meanwhile, Teresa is at last able to enjoy her son for who he is. 'I feel sad that I've only just got to know him after six and a half years,' she admitted. 'He's the same child he's always been, it's just that our relationship is different.'

POINTS TO REMEMBER

○ If you want to be an effective parent, recognize how your beliefs about yourself and your child can affect that.

○ Believe that change is possible, rather than worry that your child won't allow change to happen.

○ Look at the control you have given your child, and feel positive that you, as the adult and the parent, can regain it.

○ If you tell yourself that your child won't change his behaviour, he won't.

○ If you believe that your child is a monster, she will be.

○ Our beliefs steer our thoughts, feelings and behaviours: negative beliefs lead to negative experiences and a lack of confidence in oneself.

○ If you are anxious that your child will misbehave, and therefore avoid the situations where that is likely to occur, you will increase your anxiety by providing yourself with no evidence that situations can be mastered.

○ If you lack confidence and self-belief, your anxiety will make your child anxious, and that can trigger his difficult behaviour.

○ For your child to learn more positive behaviour you first have to adopt more positive beliefs about her, and also, most fundamentally, about yourself as her parent.

○ Your child's behaviour will change if you believe that as his parent you can change yours first.

chapter three

Get positive

WHEN *LITTLE ANGELS* TOOK TERESA ISHERWOOD ON HER FIRST VISIT TO THE playground at the end of her road with her son Dominic, she was given a few simple instructions: let Dominic play; watch him and praise him as much as you can for all the lovely, fun things he is doing; and give him lots of hugs. These weren't things she was used to doing, and Dominic clearly found being hugged and praised by his mum quite a novelty. For Teresa, though, this was a turning point – a chance to enjoy being with her son and to focus on his lively, joyful character rather than his defiance, which usually bothered her. It was the beginning of a new and positive phase.

Positive attention

It might sound obvious, but think for yourself how praise or positive feedback from someone, rather than nagging or complaining, makes you far more likely to want to do things that please them. It works for children too. Giving your child more positive attention is a very powerful way of reinforcing good behaviour.

If you're now recognizing that your child gets more attention for being naughty than being good, you have grasped a simple but funda-mental rule of behaviour change. The next step is to think in more detail about changing your own behaviour so that you can start giving more attention when things are going well and less when they aren't.

The next step

If you've been keeping a diary, as suggested in Chapter One, it should be getting clearer to you what you need to change. Have a look back at your diary, then consider the following questions:

1 Is my child told off more than he or she is praised?

2 Do I give more negative than positive feedback on my child's behaviour?

3 If my child does as she has been asked, do I rarely thank or praise her?

4 Are my expectations of my child's behaviour more negative than positive?

5 Do I nag my child to get him to do things?

6 Do I spend a lot of time shouting to get my child to do as I ask?

7 Do I see one of my children as the 'problem child'?

8 Do I believe that my child has the power and control in our relationship?

9 Do I feel powerless and anxious when I am with my child?

10 Have my child and I got into a cycle of negative behaviour that leaves us feeling unhappy and frustrated?

If you have answered yes to most of these questions, it's time to think in more detail about the negative patterns of behaviour you are in with your child and how these may be contributing to the behaviour problems.

It's often a cycle of behaviour and response, which may be similar to some of the following examples.

Example 1

Ignore good behaviour and give attention to bad behaviour ➤ more bad behaviour and less lovely behaviour

Sarah and Brian Christie had become convinced that everything five-year-old Matthew did was naughty. They had labelled him a 'bad boy' and spent all their time watching for his next bout of bad behaviour.

The Christies' behaviour tape showed that when Sarah was out with Matthew she was so convinced that he was out of control that she was constantly yelling at him to stay by her side. When they sat down for a snack she asked him not to play up and he tried to hug her; she ignored the hug and simply put him back on his seat, while still insisting he behave. When he was keeping his sister entertained by singing at dinnertime, he got shouted at. Matthew was learning that there were no rewards for behaving nicely.

Since Matthew had been labelled as bad, he also got the blame for behaviour that wasn't his fault. In one scene his father asked him to open the door for his sister, and Matthew bounced against the door over-enthusiastically, accidentally knocking his sister down. His father saw this as malicious and threatened to kick him back.

Matthew's parents were in a vicious cycle. They saw Matthew as the problem child, so they behaved negatively towards him, which triggered more negative behaviour. They believed that he was out of control, making it more likely that he would be. Sarah rarely praised Matthew: she ignored the behaviour she wanted and always found fault, thus reinforcing the behaviour she and her husband didn't want.

Example 2
Bad behaviour ≻ nagging ≻ more bad behaviour ≻ more nagging

Vicki Wells was convinced that her six-year-old son Oliver had got it in for her, and was worried by his defiance, aggression and lack of respect. But when Vicki watched the family's behaviour tape she was horrified to see how much she was nagging Oliver and constantly telling him off. Every exchange was a battle, and her tone of voice and body language showed how frustrated and tired with him she was. The more she went on at Oliver, the more provocative he seemed to become.

In one scene, Vicki had spent half an hour continually telling Oliver not to touch the plug sockets, and yet he was still touching them. This exhausting exchange revealed how much Oliver had got used to getting attention from his mother through nagging. The more irritated Vicki became, the less time and energy she had for fun, and the less lik was that Oliver would get positive attention. Vicki was both make his behaviour worse and causing it to happen m

Example 3

Anxiety about a problem behaviour ➣ giving attention to the behaviour ➣ the behaviour happening more often

Five-year-old Jessica Butler was dominating her parents Claire and Mick. Jessica, who was one of twins, had been born with mild cerebral palsy and a hole in the heart. As a result, Claire and Mick had always treated her with great care, and when she began to have tantrums would quickly give in to try to keep her calm. 'We never said no because if we did, a little bead of a tear would appear and it was, "Oh, she's getting upset... OK, you can have it,"' recalled Mick. Over time, this led to an escalation in Jessica's demanding behaviour, to the point where she had such severe tantrums that she would either vomit or her nose would bleed. Given her health problems, this would make Claire and Mick even more anxious to keep her calm, so Jessica would invariably be comforted and given more attention.

Although Jessica's health was now fine, she had learnt how to get her own way, while brother James rarely got a look-in. Claire and Mick had to recognize this. By giving her tantrums so much attention, they had made it more likely that the tantrums would not only continue, but keep escalating too. This way the vicious cycle would go on.

What these families needed to do

Each of these families was able to turn around the problem behaviour by giving their children more positive attention.

Sarah and Brian needed to relax more with Matthew, set clear consequences for the behaviour they didn't want, and praise everything they did want much more.

Vicki needed to stop noticing and nagging all the behaviour she didn't like, stop reacting so easily, and start praising the behaviour she wanted to see.

Claire and Mick needed to stop giving so much attention to the tantrums and start to motivate Jessica to enjoy behaving well.

How to be positive, part one: the rules

The general rule is that you need to reinforce as much of the behaviour that you do want by praising and encouraging your child, while ignoring the behaviour you don't want. Some people interpret this as an invitation to spoil the child. It isn't. It doesn't mean praising your child for being a pain, or letting him get away with something, such as fighting, spitting or swearing, while you lavish him with praise.

Being positive means calmly and decisively taking charge. From here on, you're the adult. You are going to decide very clearly what your limits are, what you will and won't accept, and make that clear to your child. You will also set consequences for the behaviour you will not accept, which we will explore in the next chapter. In the meantime, your aim is to motivate and encourage your child by changing the way you engage with him, so with any luck you won't be needing too many consequences. You're going to get positive.

1 Calm down

The majority of the parents who contacted *Little Angels* were feeling at the end of their tether with their children's behaviour. Their homes were often full of shouting, crying and strained relationships. The whole family was clearly trapped in a destructive pattern of behaviour that was causing them all distress.

The truth is that many people shout at their children. For many of us it can be an automatic response, particularly if you were shouted at as a child yourself. But it isn't the best way to get things done (or to get the children to listen), and often leaves both sides feeling stressed and unnecessarily worked up.

Zoë and Ian Maynard were terrified that their six-year-old son Sam was turning into an insolent and defiant monster. 'Our son is great mates with everyone else in the world – apart from us,' said Ian, while Zoë commented, 'He knows which buttons to press.' Zoë and Sam's relationship was strained and unhappy.

After filming with the family, it became apparent that it wasn't just Sam's shouting that was a problem, but Zoë's. The tape revealed how Sam's behaviour mirrored that of his mother, who was often fiery and quick on the draw. When Sam accidentally spilt apple juice, she was immediately at top volume. When Sam was upset with his younger brother Aaron for scribbling on his drawing, he used exactly the same volume and tone of voice to scream at him.

Zoë's shouting was having no impact on Sam other than teaching him how to shout back. So the strategy she was using to manage his aggressive behaviour was in fact making it worse. She was also inadvertently helping Sam to hone his arguing skills, strengthening the problem behaviour that she wanted to reduce. Only when Zoë learnt to stop going into battle did Sam's more equable side appear, and he stopped shouting at her too. It became easier to get him to cooperate. 'We didn't realize how stressed and wired he was,' admitted Zoë.

Zoë and Ian had also used smacking as a way of showing the boys they meant business, without realizing that this was encouraging their sons to smack each other. There was a chain reaction going through the house, as Zoë smacked Sam, Sam smacked Aaron, and Aaron kicked the cat. Aaron then got smacked by Zoë for doing so. Smacking clearly wasn't working.

Alev Huseyin was caught in a similar negative pattern of shouting at and smacking her three-year-old daughter Ayla. Alev was devastated when viewing her behaviour tape to see a screaming argument between herself and Ayla, whom she had been unsuccessfully trying to get dressed. When Ayla lashed out at her mother, Alev hit her back, shouting, 'You don't hit Mummy!' The argument got worse. 'I don't like smacking my kids,' sobbed Alev, 'they don't deserve to be treated that way.' All Alev was doing was reinforcing smacking and shouting as a way of behaving.

The rule: If you want your child's behaviour to settle down, remain calm. Shout and you will teach them to shout. Hit them and you will teach them to hit. Try taking a step back.

2 Don't engage
Vicki Wells was convinced that Oliver was trying to wind her up with insults, such as telling her, 'I'm going to kill you with a rusty knife'.

She would get angry and argue with him, but found his defiance and cheekiness difficult to manage, especially as he would often answer her back. 'He's trying to do everything to wind me up,' she said. 'When he doesn't get his own way he will snap and physically elbow me in aggression. It's something I feel I almost can't cope with any more.'

Vicki's strong reaction had taught Oliver that his rude behaviour was the best way to get attention from her, so their negative interactions became the main part of their relationship.

Once Vicki was able to take a step back and look at her own behaviour, she was able to see how much she was contributing to the ongoing battle. 'It took me looking at that video to realize how negative I was. It's completely turned things around,' she said. During her first session with the earpiece, Vicki was challenged to put up a tent in the garden with Oliver, without reacting to anything that might usually cause a row. When Oliver tried to grab a tent pole she firmly took it back from him without a fuss; when he became abusive she just let it wash over her. Without any attention for his usual rudeness, Oliver soon tired of this tack and gave up. The more relaxed Vicki got, the less mileage there was for Oliver in being a pain.

Afterwards Vicki reflected how much of a difference staying calm and not engaging with irritating behaviour had made. 'I used to just lose it automatically at the first instant,' she realized. Following the tent episode, she began to notice how Oliver's anger seemed to have disappeared – because she wasn't getting angry with him.

Of course children can wind you up, but the more attention you give for the behaviour that provokes you, the more likely you are to get that behaviour. While none of us wants to sit back and let a child be abusive to us, it's important to think through what it is you really need to react to and set limits around what you will accept.

The desire to have the last word is in all of us, but keep reminding yourself that you are the grown-up in any argument. Melissa Christoforou would get drawn into arguments with her eight-year-old daughter Indianna, during which they traded equally childish insults. The arguments could have been defused much earlier if Melissa had just ignored the childishness.

As many children watch a lot of television, their verbal abilities can be more sophisticated than their actual understanding, and lead parents to have expectations of behaviour that is way beyond their age and development. This leads to over-negotiating and arguing with them as if they were adults. It's important to recognize that your child isn't actually setting out to wind you up. Young children do not have the ability to premeditate their behaviour, except on a very basic level relating to what they know will get them the most attention.

All the attention you give your children by negotiating and arguing will make them more likely to argue and answer back. Meanwhile, their increased bad behaviour will strengthen your belief that they are trying to wind you up. Thus the battle rages on and on.

The rule: Do not engage in a battle with your children because you think they are out to get you. Remember that you are the adult.

3 Praise and praise again

The expression 'glowing with praise' exists for good reason. It may seem obvious, but praising your children more than you criticize or tell them off is the best way of getting what you want. It's that simple, but something that many of the *Little Angels* parents weren't doing.

When we started filming with the Christie family, Sarah and Brian were so stressed by Matthew's defiance that many of their interactions with him were exasperated and critical. It was a surprise for them to be taken to the park to play instead of being offered some strategies for discipline.

All Sarah and Brian were asked to do was follow Matthew's play, commenting on what he was doing and praising him for everything he did on the climbing frame and slide. Matthew immediately responded to the praise, and was soon leaping into their arms for hugs and kisses. It was a moving moment for his parents, who suddenly saw how praise helped bring out the wonderful, warm side of him they feared they would never see. The experience of positive time with Matthew enabled them to begin to make the leap in changing their view of him. 'It's given me a different way of looking at things,' Brian Christie later commented. 'It's been one of the best things we've ever done for Matthew,' agreed Sarah.

The main thing to remember about praising your children is to try to do it regularly. Praise them for doing the things you ask them to do, as well as for things they spontaneously remember to do on their own. If they are sitting quietly getting on with a game, you can praise them for playing nicely. Several times a day for no reason at all just grab them and give them a big hug and tell them how lovely they are being: this is called *positive practice*. Don't worry that you'll spoil them. You're offering a positive reward for positive behaviour.

The rule: Praise the behaviour you want and you'll get more of it. Ignore what you don't like and it will soon diminish from lack of attention.

4 Use distraction

As you get more familiar with some of the behaviour patterns recorded in your diaries, you may come to recognize some of the triggers to bad behaviour. As children have such a short attention span, a positive way to avoid problems is to distract them before anything happens.

Jane Soilleux used to dread taking her three-year-old daughter Emily to the supermarket as Emily's tantrums made it a struggle to get anything done. During an earpiece session in the supermarket, Jane was shown how she could avoid a tantrum by catching it before it started. As Emily began to tune up, Jane pointed to the ceiling and said, 'Oh, my goodness, what's up there? Can you see the bird? You look up there and tell me when you can see it.' It was enough to stop Emily in her tracks. By the time she'd looked up and imagined that she too had seen the bird, she'd forgotten what she was getting worked up about.

With distraction and praise for helping Jane shop, a situation that would usually end in tears became enjoyable. 'Normally I feel guilty bringing her shopping because she doesn't like it,' said Jane. But this time had been different. 'I don't feel like I've done a hard day's work, and I think Emily's enjoyed it more.'

It's possible to distract younger children with just about anything; you can let your imagination run riot. If they're getting locked into an argument with you, or demanding something you don't want to give them, just try changing the subject. If that doesn't work, create any distraction you like, from a dinosaur in the garden to a spot on the carpet. Your child's attention will be drawn immediately to whatever it is you're suggesting, and often this will be enough to move them on.

Lisa Williams felt she could never go out with four-year-old Kieran. 'If I did take him into a field with a ball, I know there'd be a tantrum coming home,' she complained. So Lisa was taught via an earpiece how to use distraction to get him home.

She and Kieran played together by a lake, and when it was time to leave Lisa had to get him away without once mentioning that they were leaving. 'Oh look, did you see that squirrel?' she said, and then walked away without looking back. Kieran quickly followed her. Now she had to think of the next thing she could distract him with. 'Ooh,' she said, 'are those blackberries up there?' And he followed her a bit further. By tempting him with a new distraction every few minutes, Lisa successfully lured Kieran away without any protest. As he was completely preoccupied with what they were doing, he had no reason to behave badly.

The rule: Try to distract your children away from problem behaviour if you see it approaching. If you can't distract them from their behaviour, distract yourself from getting wound up.

5 Be playful

For many of the parents who took part in *Little Angels* the problems with their children had completely overshadowed any of the more pleasurable time they had spent together. They had forgotten how much fun their children could be.

Children enjoy life without the pressures that we have to deal with, and this can be a wonderful antidote to our stress. Play is an important aspect of child development, and many studies have shown the value of play in improving bonding between parents and children.

It's easy to spend the time you could be having fun with your children leaving them in front of the TV while you get on with chores.

Ask yourself how often your children become just another responsibility among the many things that have to be done each day. If, like Zora Lunniss, you view your children and their needs as a series of tasks to get through, the chances are you are not enjoying them and that you probably have more difficult than happy times with them.

Zora felt that every day with her three-year-old twins Asha and Elodie was an uphill struggle. This was having a negative impact on her mood and she was becoming increasingly unhappy. One problem for Zora was that she hated mess of any kind, so when the girls had toys and crayons out, she would run around clearing up after them rather than enjoying their play.

Zora was set a play session with her girls, which included making lots of mess with paints in the garden. She was asked to interact with the twins by really exaggerating her praise and smiles, and when one twin had an inevitable tantrum, she had to ignore that while concentrating on the twin who was playing nicely. Zora got really involved in finger-painting with Elodie, making handprints and even painting her face. By relaxing into the play, and focusing on the good behaviour instead of the screaming, she had a revelation. 'I did feel it worked,' she said. 'She really seemed to enjoy it, and I actually started to enjoy it, which I didn't think I would.'

When playing with your children, try to let them lead the play as much as you can. Ask them what they want to play, rather than making suggestions yourself. As they play, try making a running commentary on what they are doing in really positive terms. This shows your child that you are paying attention. Also praise them for what they are doing and how well they are doing it. If you try to control things too much, they may feel that this is another way of you laying down the law.

Lisa Williams had got into such a negative interaction with Kieran that she was shown how to play with him by letting him paint her face. She was forbidden from making any negative comments or telling him what he should be doing. The brush proved rather tickly for her, but Kieran loved it.

Even if you can't make much time for playing, it's important to incorporate play and playfulness into as many of your everyday activities as you can. If you have a task to accomplish, try to do it by being playful. For example:

○ Sarah Christie kept Matthew preoccupied while shopping with a game to find cards for relatives.

○ Tamara Carrera got Keanu to clear up his toys by making it into a race between them to see who could pick them up first.

○ The three Price children were stopped from getting upset at losing a card game when Nigel and Bianca told them funny stories to distract them.

The rule: Be creative with your parenting. Think of ways of engaging your children in tasks they don't want to do, or distract them from bad behaviour. Children become fun if they're having fun.

6 Get organized

As a broad rule, children are real sticklers for routine: they like to know where they stand and what is happening when. If your family life is chaotic, it may be harder for you to make specific changes around issues such as sleeping, eating or behaviour. So, where possible, try to streamline your routines to make family life easier.

Life was chaos for Matt and Mandie Elson and their five children. Matt was trying to work from home while informally looking after their three-year-old triplets, and although his wife Mandie was also at home, neither of them had clearly defined their roles. Although they wanted to sort out issues around sleeping and discipline, Matt and Mandie were asked to look first at their routine to create a better-functioning and happier household. They had to agree a daily schedule of tasks so that Matt knew when he could have long periods of uninterrupted work time, and Mandie knew when she could call on him to support her at the busiest and most problematic times of day. Their new schedule showed an hour-by-hour breakdown of their day, and was pinned up in the kitchen.

Following this, they were able to look at the sleeping and eating routines they had for the children. Soon the daily structure of family life felt better managed, and the routines introduced a calmer, more organized atmosphere to the household. Specific behavioural changes then became easier.

The rule: Try to define specific times for meals and bedtimes, and work out a division of labour between parents. If children are clear about what is happening, they will feel happier.

7 Get them out

Like Sue Angell, many parents with children who behave badly fall into the vicious cycle of never taking them out for fear that they'll mis-behave. This in turn means that the children don't have the stimulation of getting out enough, which means they are more likely to behave badly at home, and so it goes on.

Children thrive on fresh air and physical exercise. If they are driving you mad indoors, the best thing you can do is get them out. Take them to a park or any area where they can expend some of their limitless supplies of energy, and if you're feeling fraught, you can cool off too. The deafening noise that children can make is always more bearable outdoors.

You don't need to plan wildly complicated outings. Small children will enjoy going to feed the ducks, a walk to the local swings, or just going to throw a ball around the nearest patch of green space. Yvette Edwards was getting very stressed by the refusal of three-year-old Yssis to eat her meals. A simple outing to have a picnic in a local park gave Yvette and Yssis a chance to spend some relaxed time together, as well as an opportunity to have some fun with food.

Tracy Ellmore couldn't cope with taking out her three-year-old triplets Rio, India and Carlo, as she was terrified that she wouldn't be able to control them and one of them would get hurt. Stuck at home all the time, the triplets were going wild, tearing the wallpaper off in strips and climbing every available surface in the house. Tracy had to learn how to take charge by clearly communicating with them not to run away and when to come back. On early trips out she used wrist reins to teach the triplets that if they didn't stay near her, they had to be on the reins. The triplets quickly learnt to come back when asked, and Tracy felt calmer and more in control. Once she started getting the children out more, her confidence increased and the children got more exercise. Tracy's horizons also expanded, as they were able to do more things together as a family.

The rule: If in doubt, get them out.

How to be positive, part two: motivation

Most of the *Little Angels* families felt they had 'tried everything' and ended up defeated. Their children, they believed, were beyond conventional help. Most universally criticized was the sticker chart. As one parent said, 'The sticker charts worked for a week, then the kids lost interest in them.'

The truth is that sticker charts don't work if you don't use them consistently. If you do, they are a fun and visual way of offering your children the incentive to do well and behave more positively. They give them another layer of praise and encouragement for their good behaviour, while more developed charts can also allow children to earn rewards for timed periods of good behaviour.

To help you use sticker charts properly and consistently, look at the following examples we used with some of our *Little Angels* families.

Luke Barton's chart

Luke's behaviour was defiant and wilful. He would never do as he was told, and his parents Jo and Jason would spend ages arguing and negotiating with him. As they began to praise him more than they argued with him, they needed to offer him an incentive to change his behaviour as well. Opposite is an example of their simple but effective chart, divided into three-hour time slots.

Time	Mon	Tue	Wed	Thu	Fri	Sat	Sun
07.00–10.00	★	★					
10.00–13.00	★☹	★					
13.00–16.00	★	★☹					
16.00–19.00	★	☹☹ ✗					

These were the instructions for Jo and Jason:

○ For every three-hour period that Luke was well behaved, he got a sticker (we've used stars above) in the appropriate slot. This was done in front of him with lots of praise.

○ If he behaved badly, he was given two chances to change his behaviour – once by being asked nicely to stop what he was doing, then once being asked firmly (this is dealt with in more detail in Chapter Four).

○ If Luke did not do as he was told, he would watch a sad face being drawn on the chart.

○ If, at the end of the time period, he had only one sad face, a sticker (star) would be placed over it (all children are naughty at times).

○ If he had two or more sad faces in the slot a big, black cross would be drawn through the slot.

○ Luke was told that if he got three out of four possible stickers (stars) every day, he would get a special treat before bedtime. A slot with a black cross in it counted as a lost slot, and he knew he could have only one of these per day if he wanted his treat.

○ The treat would be special time alone with either parent – perhaps playing a quiet game or reading a comic with them.

Within a week, Luke's behaviour had become much more positive. He quickly learnt that he wanted to avoid sad faces and black crosses at all costs, and even put his hand over the chart to try to stop his father writing on it. This was a powerful way of changing his behaviour. The success of the chart meant that Jo also took a portable version of it when she went shopping with all three of her boys.

Matthew Christie's chart

Matthew, aged five, was defiant, wilful and aggressive. His sticker chart was very similar to Luke's, but to begin with we focused on 10-minute time periods for him to be well behaved. Smaller time slots also gave him a greater chance of succeeding. Sarah found the period between teatime and bathtime particularly stressful, so we started there. The rules around Matthew's chart were the same as for Luke except:

○ If he was aggressive, he would be put into his room for five minutes – one minute for each year of his life. This is called 'time out' and is covered in Chapter Four.

Time	Mon	Tue	Wed	Thu	Fri	Sat	Sun
17.00– 17.10	★	★					
17.10– 17.20	☹ ☹	★					
17.20– 17.30	☹ ☹	☹					
17.30– 17.40	☹	time out					
17.40– 17.50	★	★					
17.50– 18.00	★	★					

○ Two sad faces = a black cross in the slot, so the slot is lost.
○ Time out also = a black cross in the slot, so the slot is lost.
○ Four out of six slots stickered (starred) per hour session = a treat at the end of the day.

It may seem that Matthew was getting an easier time than Luke, but his chart would have been just as hard for him. Matthew's chart reflected the level of bad behaviour, which was more extreme than Luke's. In order for you to decide which chart to use, look at the B column of your diary. If the bad behaviour happens extremely frequently every day, work out the most difficult time of day and start there. For the rest of the time, practise ignoring irritating behaviour as much as possible. Praise based around the sticker chart, in contrast to being ignored, will give your children a very clear message about how they can behave to get the best out of you.

Jay Cooper's chart

Seven-year-old Jay Cooper would fight very aggressively with his brother Owen, and his mother Kathy was terrified that he might cause him a serious injury. The atmosphere in the house was very tense and unhappy. As a young child, Jay had witnessed the physical abuse of his mother, and his fighting reflected this. His self esteem was also very low. The sticker chart for him and his five-year-old brother needed to be full of fun, and something that they could succeed at. Their chart and rules were very similar to Matthew Christie's, but their whole day was split into 10-minute slots. As they were at school for most of the day, this was manageable during the week, but weekends were very busy sticker times for Kathy and her partner Jamie. They also had some additional rules:

○ To increase the fun and the incentive to behave well, each boy was given a marbles jar to paint. At the end of the day they could count up their stickered time slots and count the same number of brightly coloured marbles into their jars.

○ An agreed number of marbles meant a treat at the end of the day (e.g. time with parents, cuddles and play).

○ If they wanted, they could also save up marbles and exchange them for bigger treats, such as an outing to the joke shop – a great favourite with the boys.

Kathy and Jamie worked really hard at the charts, and combined them with lots of praise and cuddles. Jay's behaviour improved quickly, and the fighting significantly decreased. Jay also enjoyed having the currency of his marbles, and being able to save and exchange them.

The Elson, Price and Georgiou charts

You can also design sticker charts around specific problem behaviour in order to give the children the incentive to improve:

○ The triplets Velvet, Bayley and Romany Elson each had a sleep sticker chart (see page 95).

○ The three Price children, Miles, Herbie and Ella, had a sticker chart designed around their mealtime behaviour (see page 119).

○ Nicola Georgiou had a chart designed to motivate her to go to the toilet rather than wet herself (see page 133).

BASIC RULES OF STICKER CHARTS

○ Sticker charts work only with children aged over three; below that age, children don't really understand the concept. If you are trying a chart with an older child, make one for younger siblings too, as the spirit of competition may help the older child to engage with it.

○ Involve your children in making the sticker chart: let them decorate it and feel as though it positively belongs to them rather than some-thing negative being done to them. Children love stickers, so get them involved in choosing which ones to buy.

○ Treats should not be food. Your time and cuddles, reading and playing together are healthier and more powerful rewards.

○ As your child does well, build up the difficulty each week by increas-ing the duration of each time slot.

○ You could also let your children know that if they manage three days of success in a row, they could have a bigger treat, such as a trip to the cinema, as well as their daily small treats.

❍ At the end of the day, if the children have done well, have a big family cheer around the sticker chart.

❍ If they don't achieve all their slots, be calm and suggest that they might do better tomorrow, but leave it at that. Remember, ignore what you don't want and don't make too much fuss over it.

❍ If your children are struggling to achieve their slots, maybe you have set too high a standard. Try cutting back to what they can achieve, even if it means sticking with half an hour per day of five-minute slots. Success will lead to small shifts in behaviour, which you can then build on.

❍ Sticker charts not only motivate children and offer them incentives to change their behaviour, but also train you to keep positively focused on what they are doing well.

❍ As your relationship with your child improves, and there are more praise and cuddles than shouting and nagging, the sticker chart will become redundant and your child will lose interest. At that point, but not before, you can phase it out. If you lose interest first, you can expect it not to work.

Words of caution

Before you read on to the chapters that outline the specific techniques for behaviour change, it's important that you have understood three things:

❍ That your behaviour is as much of a problem as your child's.

❍ That in order for your child to change, you have to believe that you can change first.

❍ That only positive beliefs about yourself and your child, and a positive approach to his or her behaviour, will ensure success.

Even if you now feel ready to move on in a positive way, always remember that:

❍ Change takes time.

○ Things often get worse before they get better; children will kick against new boundaries.

○ If you are not consistent in your approach over weeks rather than days, the approach will fail.

○ If you are not united with others who parent with you, your child will get a mixed message and be unable to change his or her behaviour.

POINTS TO REMEMBER

In order to get more positive behaviour, parents must start by being positive themselves. Focus on your child's best qualities, then adopt the following rules.

○ Stay calm: behave in the way you would like your children to.

○ Don't engage and argue back, unless you want to teach children how to argue better.

○ Use imagination and games to distract away from the problem. Having fun at tricky times can often prevent bad behaviour.

○ Praise more than you criticize.

○ Use play to engage your children in a difficult task: it will make life a lot easier.

○ Use sticker charts and reward systems to motivate and encourage good behaviour. It works if you start in a way that is achievable for you and your child, then stick to it.

○ Plan realistic routines and activities. Children feel settled by clear routines, and behaviour improves.

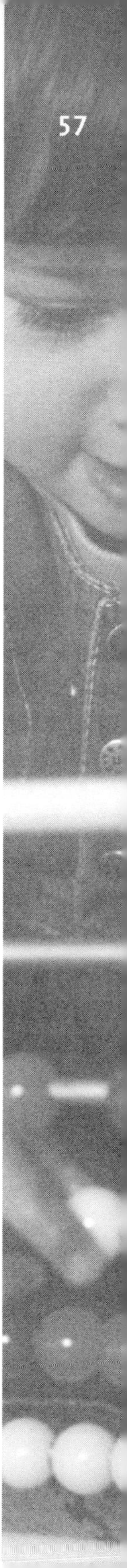

chapter four

The bottom line

IN AN IDEAL WORLD CHILDREN WILL DO AS YOU ASK THE FIRST TIME YOU ASK THEM, and stop doing the things you don't want them to the moment you say. In reality, children are always going to test you far more than that. Being positive and creative in your approach will make life much easier, but you will also need to decide where you want to draw the line with your children's behaviour, and what you will and won't accept.

Many of the families who took part in *Little Angels* were keen for us to give them rules to follow. We, on the other hand, wanted the parents to define for themselves precisely what they wanted. After that they had a choice of strategies they could use to ensure they got it. So now is a good point for you to think about how you would like to set limits around your children's behaviour. It is time to set some boundaries.

Boundaries

When we first met four-year-old Nicola Georgiou her behaviour was out of control. She was screaming, shouting and hitting to force her mother Christina to continue letting her breastfeed. Christina was beginning to think that she had a child who was beyond help. But Nicola had not been given a clear sense of boundaries.

All children need clear boundaries in order to understand the rules around their behaviour. With boundaries in place, their behaviour is more likely to settle.

○ Boundaries make expectations clear, so children know where they stand.

○ Boundaries reduce uncertainty and anxiety for both parents and children, thus keeping behaviour calm.

All families are different. We each have our own experiences, backgrounds and cultural beliefs, so it's for you and your family to decide what your boundaries are going to be. (This is discussed in more detail on pages 61–2.)

Consequences

Whatever you decide your limits are, they become real only when put into action. In other words, children need to know what the consequences of their behaviour are. For younger children in particular, actions speak far louder than words.

The principles of being positive are:

○ Good behaviour ➤ praise ➤ more good behaviour

○ Bad behaviour ➤ ignore ➤ less bad behaviour

The clear rule about behaviour is that the response you give *immediately* after it has occurred will be extremely powerful in determining whether that behaviour is continued, maintained or reduced.

A united front

Some families have one parent, others have two, and some have step-parenting relationships. Whatever your situation, if you are co-parenting your child with anyone else, it's vital that you are in agreement and backing each other up. When couples are not in agreement about what they want, it is extremely hard to set clear boundaries around behaviour.

In some of the two-parent families we met, the challenge we often faced was in trying to reconcile the differing expectations the parents had about their children's behaviour. Such differences sometimes led parents to manage the children differently, and even to argue in front of them. This meant that the children had no clarity about what was expected from them, so it made their behaviour worse.

We saw this with three-year-old Ayla Huseyin, whom we filmed having lunch with her parents in a restaurant. Her mother Alev wouldn't let Ayla have ice cream because she hadn't eaten her main course. Ayla cried, and her father Somer 'felt sorry for her' and fetched her an ice cream. Father and daughter exchanged knowing smiles, and Ayla muttered, 'Stupid Mummy' to Somer, who openly laughed. The consequence was that Somer undermined his wife's authority in front of Ayla, making his daughter more powerful than her mother. Meanwhile, Ayla learnt that she could behave badly and still get what she wanted.

Deciding on your boundaries

Nigel and Bianca Price were another set of parents who disagreed about the rules of the house. Bianca felt Nigel was too tough and disciplinarian, while Nigel saw Bianca as a 'soft touch'. During the making of Little Angels, they were taken to a café (a neutral place stops you having arguments in the same way as you might at home) to try to agree boundaries around their children's behaviour.

They agreed that Bianca would try to be firmer with the children so that no really meant no. Nigel agreed to try not to shout at her or the children when he became frustrated by their behaviour. They then drew up a charter for their children, which included:

Behaviour:
- No fighting.
- No biting, scratching or drawing blood.
- No answering back or swearing.

Mealtimes:
- Sitting on a chair at the table and not getting off it.
- Eating unaided, using a knife and fork.
- Getting pudding only after eating all the main course.

Having agreed on all these points, they were able to go home and start working together on presenting a more united front.

HOW TO SET BOUNDARIES

In order for you to start some clear boundary setting, both you and (if appropriate) your partner can do the following exercise.

○ List all the problem behaviour that exists in your family (yours and your children's).

○ Try to organize the problems into larger groups, e.g. behaviour, sleeping, eating, etc.

○ Rank them in order of priority – the most urgent to change at the top.

○ Go through each problem and write out what you would ideally like to see happening differently.

○ Check your list and make sure that it is realistic and you are not expecting perfection – children are children, after all.

○ If you are parenting as a couple, look at your lists and negotiate so that each ideal behaviour is defined in a way that feels acceptable to both of you. Remember, you may both need to compromise.

○ Write out your Parent's Charter in clear, positive phrases so that you can refer back to it in times of stress or potential disagreement.

As you do this task, remember to refer back to your diary, particularly the C column. This will enable you to see how the consequences you give to your child's behaviour can lack clarity and lead to unclear boundaries. You may be able to see how differing styles of parenting contribute to the lack of clarity.

If your children are six or over, you might prefer to negotiate a family contract with them present. You can agree the behaviour you want and the consequences for the behaviour you don't want (see page 66). We don't recommend doing this with children younger than six.

Strategies for getting what you want

Once you have drawn up a list of boundaries, you can think about how you are going to achieve them. Remember, these approaches will work best in a warm, loving and happy environment where your child also receives a lot of positive attention. Then you can think about using the following strategies to give your child clear messages.

Be clear what you want

In the Price family behaviour tape we saw how it took Nigel 15 minutes to get a screaming five-year-old Herbie into the bath, while yelling, 'Get in there now! Get in there now! I don't care if you want a bath or not!' Nigel's temper quickly escalated to loud shouting; later Bianca gently comforted a still-tearful Herbie, telling him he was 'being silly'. The two parents' differing approaches were making Herbie more powerful, as he got lots of attention for being awkward, but he wasn't getting a clear message from his parents about the behaviour they expected.

Many of the *Little Angels* families felt frustrated that they could not get their children to do what they wanted. During their behaviour tape sessions, it would often become clear that one of the main reasons for this was that their children did not have a clear message about the rules governing their behaviour. A key task for Tanya, Stephen and Rachel was to help the parents define boundaries and learn techniques for setting them clearly in place.

Mick and Claire Butler were taught about giving the children a clear message on a family outing with their five-year-old twins James and Jessica. The plan was for Claire and Mick to take Polaroid photos of moments when the twins were being good in order to reinforce what is meant by good behaviour. During a game of football, James got angry and tried to hit his father. He was clearly told that if he did that again, he'd have to stop playing; when he sulked he was ignored, while the game went on without him.

By excluding James from the game and meanwhile taking more pictures of well-behaved Jessica having fun, Claire and Mick showed James that there were new rules being set down. They were giving him a powerful message: if you throw a tantrum, you won't have fun. Eventually, James returned to the game and the children went home happily, which was a new experience for Claire. 'We're normally ready to kill them by now and dragging them home!' she laughed. By giving a clear message whenever the twins were badly behaved, Claire and Mick were setting new boundaries. From now on bad behaviour would get no rewards.

Get what you ask for

'They don't listen to me at all,' Tracy Ellmore said of her three-year-old triplets. 'They just run away and don't bother to listen.' She was sick of the sound of her own voice. 'My neighbours hate it because I'm constantly shouting, "Don't do this, don't do that, that's enough, I've had enough now, all of you just go away!"'

Being ignored by their children when they wanted them to do something was a common problem for many of the *Little Angels* families. Kathy Cooper would ask her sons Jay and Owen to do things over and over again, and they still wouldn't cooperate. Tamara Carrera nagged her four-year-old Keanu to the extent that he thought that was her normal voice, and ignored her. Mandie Elson was constantly shouting at her five children and getting nowhere. Somehow the commands weren't getting through.

Think about how you ask your children to do things, then ask yourself these key questions:

○ Do I ask more than twice?
○ Do I yell my instructions from the outset?
○ Do I sound like I don't really mean it?

If you have answered yes to any of these questions, you a) nag, or b) shout too much, or c) lack authority.

Show you mean business

On *Little Angels* we asked parents to adopt a rule when speaking to their children: never ask them more than twice. If you keep asking your children, they will learn to ignore you. If you shout, they will become immune to your anger. If your voice lacks authority, they will not take you seriously. In order to get your children to do as they are asked, you need to ask them once nicely, then once again, firmly.

Ask once nicely

○ Use a tone of voice that is calm and friendly but conveys authority.
○ Make sure you can be heard and that you are making eye contact with your child.
○ Speak to your child as you would like to be spoken to when being asked to do something.

If your child does as you have asked, respond positively, with lots of praise and thanks. We suggested that *Little Angels* parents show how pleased they were by responding with the exaggerated enthusiasm of children's party entertainers. If your child refuses or ignores you, it's time to be firmer.

Ask once firmly

○ Move closer to your child, get down on to his level and make clear eye contact with him.
○ Your tone of voice should be calm, but show that you mean business.
○ Increase your volume in order to command attention, but don't shout, as that means you are losing control.
○ Your body language should be focused towards your child, and everything about you should say to him that you're in charge.

Again, if your child does as you have asked, give her lots of thanks and praise. Even if she did it only after being asked a second time, the point is that she did it. With consistent praise from you over time, she will soon be doing as requested the first time she is asked.

Five-year-old Owen and seven-year-old Jay Cooper would take no notice of their mother Kathy while she constantly nagged them; tension and unhappiness in the household were spiralling. Kathy was shown how to use her tone of voice and body language to convey a real sense of authority to the boys, which would make them take her more seriously. Kathy then had to put it to the test at a children's play centre by giving the boys clear instructions when it was time to leave. She succeeded, and later reflected how clearer boundaries were helping her to enjoy her sons far more. 'For the first time I can't wait to pick them up from school, and I really miss them during the day,' she admitted.

Mandie Elson also felt that her five children didn't listen to anything she said. She shouted all the time, but the attention the children got from the shouting was just reinforcing their bad behaviour. After working on her new assertive voice, Mandie went on a family picnic to practise being more authoritative. Her son Tannar began throwing pine cones at her, and she was able to ask him calmly and firmly to stop before the situation escalated. She was able to control the children far more easily by setting ground rules for the picnic and giving firm, clear commands.

Impose consequences

If you have twice asked your child to do something and he still doesn't do it, you will need to impose a consequence that shows you're not happy with his lack of cooperation. You have several choices here: you may choose to ignore him, withhold rewards, or opt for time out.

While you need to be consistent, it's important not to get too fixated on situations that aren't worth making a stand on. Decide what you will not tolerate and what you are prepared to let pass. Life is never perfect, and in the course of a day there may be things you'll find you're prepared to let go. Choose your battles. Vicki Wells had got so caught up in fighting over every little thing with six-year-old Oliver that when she asked him twice to put his shoes on, and he didn't, she decided not to make a big thing of it. She was keen to get the children out of the house, and simply decided that in the grand scheme of things this incident wasn't worth a fight. So she helped him put his shoes on and moments later they were out enjoying themselves.

Ignoring

A powerful technique that gives your children the message that their bad behaviour will not be tolerated is to ignore them. Many parents say that they have tried this but it doesn't work. This is often because they have buckled and given in to their children's demands rather than braving it out to the bitter end.

The purpose of ignoring is to give the undesirable behaviour no attention, and thus make it happen much less often. Combine this with all your praise for the wonderful behaviour, and your child will soon realize that there's nothing to be gained from bad behaviour.

Tamara Carrera was trying to get four-year-old Keanu to clear up, when he became aggressive and started throwing toys around. Tamara was told to ignore him and make it clear that she was not happy with his behaviour, saying, 'I will not talk to you until you tidy up.' Not used to being ignored, Keanu became very physical, hitting his mother and trying to make her talk to him. Tamara walked away from him, saying only, 'I will talk to you when you do what I've asked you to do.' Although Keanu persisted for some time, he eventually calmed down, having been shown he would get no attention for being difficult.

Sam and Tim Norris were unable to deal with three-year-old Katie's defiance and tantrums. Like many other parents, they believed that ignoring didn't work, and would negotiate with Katie to try to calm the tantrums. This, however, was only making them worse. Sam and Tim were taken shopping wearing earpieces to learn how to show Katie that they were in control.

Katie quickly began to play up while Sam was looking for a pair of trousers to buy. The tears began as soon as she was asked to stop running around and take her father's hand. Katie tried to take control by insisting she wanted to hold her mother's hand, but Tim was told not to give in to her, and to keep holding her firmly. His instinct was to bend down to Katie's level and engage with her, but he was discouraged from talking to her while she was screaming. The tantrum continued as they walked out of the shop, but Tim had to keep going and not allow her behaviour to control his. He walked with her crying and resisting all the way up the street and into a pizza restaurant.

Sam and Tim managed to keep ignoring Katie as she went on screaming in the restaurant, which was particularly hard as they were in public and having to brave the looks of others. It was also a real challenge sitting so close to her, as she could pull at Tim's sleeves and stretch her arms out to Sam. But they managed not to engage with her, and after a long 10 minutes Katie's tantrum stopped and she ate her meal as if nothing had happened. Sam and Tim began to recognize how powerful ignoring could be.

Some parents won't ignore because they think:
- It's too tiring or stressful to keep up.
- It makes children behave worse.
- If out in public, everyone will stare at you.

Good reasons for ignoring:
- Although hard work in the short term, ignoring will benefit you in the long term, as your child's behaviour improves and your relationship becomes more fun.
- Yelling is just as tiring and makes the bad behaviour more likely to happen.
- Nothing worthwhile is achieved without effort.
- People who are staring may have been in the same position themselves; or they don't have children and can't understand.
- Children's behaviour often gets worse as they kick against new boundaries. This is when parents give up. Don't! With calm perseverance and consistency, it will get better.

No means no

Children's tears can trigger all sorts of emotions in us, and many parents told us that they couldn't bear to see their children upset. But showing you mean business involves knowing when to say no and sticking to it. Giving in to tantrums and tears allows your child to think, 'If I really go on and on about something, I can get what I want.' If you try to justify yourself by saying you have given in 'to keep the peace', you have actually had the opposite effect.

Christina Georgiou had been trying to stop Nicola breastfeeding since she was two. She had repeatedly told her now four-year-old daughter that she no longer wished her to breastfeed. But despite being told no, Nicola had learnt that if she forced herself on her mother whenever she sat and made a phone call, Christina would give in. There were frequent arguments between them as Nicola continued to get her own way. Nicola's increasing aggression when being told no left Christina feeling powerless to impose her own will for fear of a worse tantrum. Thus the cycle went on.

Three-year-old twins Elodie and Asha Lunniss had also learnt that if they screamed long enough and hard enough, their mother Zora would give in to their demands. Zora was working hard at trying to ignore difficult behaviour when they demanded biscuits before lunch. As she tried to stand firm, they gave her a deafening stereo performance, until Zora eventually caved in to their screams and handed out the biscuits. 'I couldn't bear it any longer,' Zora admitted. 'They just weren't going to back down, and it could have gone on for hours.'

The tough message is that every time you give in, the behaviour you've given in to is more likely to make a return visit. So when you want to say no to your child, it's worth gritting your teeth and standing firm.

No rewards

Many parents use the 'If you don't do x, you won't get y' tactic. This can all too easily turn into empty and unrealistic threats. Children know only too well that you're unlikely to follow through on threats such as, 'If you don't stop doing that, I'll cancel the holiday'. Whenever you make a threat that doesn't materialize it simply reinforces children's bad behaviour and means they won't take you seriously.

Denying rewards or privileges can, however, be a very effective strategy. If you are using a sticker chart and ignoring does not work, withholding a reward can be a powerful back-up technique. Luke Barton and Matthew Christie would be asked once nicely, then once firmly to stop what they were doing. If they did not stop, they would lose the opportunity to earn a sticker, and their parents would draw a sad face on the chart. Too many of these, and their end-of-the-day reward would be lost.

With older children who have the capacity to understand the longer-term implications of their behaviour, you can use a strategy where things are taken away as a consequence of bad behaviour. This can be agreed in advance with your children so that they have a clear idea of your expectations and the likely penalties.

Matt and Mandie Elson drew up a penalty chart with nine-year-old Shelby and seven-year-old Tannar, and agreed that they would lose time on their prized Play Station if they fought. The chart divided their daily half-hour of Play Station time into six slots of five minutes each. Every time either boy behaved badly a cross would be marked on the chart and he would lose his time. This worked well because neither boy wanted to lose more time than his brother, so a competitive spirit kept their behaviour on track. This approach is an effective way of reducing rows, and also reinforces the concept that if you do what is asked, you are more likely to get what you want.

Actions not words

The most important point to remember with children, especially younger ones, is that actions speak louder than words. Many of the *Little Angels* parents would spend hours arguing and negotiating with their children, unwittingly fuelling their bad behaviour. The best way to teach children about the behaviour you don't want is to show them with a minimum of fuss.

When Oliver Wells took a tent pole that his mother Vicki didn't want him to play with, she started to negotiate with him to get it back. What she needed to do was tell him firmly that he couldn't play with it, then simply take it back. Similarly, when Emily Soilleux started struggling and fussing about getting into the shopping trolley, the best thing her mother Jane could do was put her in without any discussion. By clearly showing your children what you want, you are helping them to learn that you mean what you say.

Sarah Christie was out shopping with five-year-old Matthew when he decided to make a run for it. She had to chase him around the shop to catch him, but once she had done so, she was told to show him that he had behaved badly with actions rather than words. She marched him firmly and without any discussion straight out of the shop; she then sat on a bench and held him on her lap without speaking to him until he had calmed down. Matthew was given several clear messages: that Sarah was not happy with his behaviour, that she was in charge, and that there was no reward for running away.

SMACKING

While smacking might be action rather than words, we don't recommend it as a technique for managing children's behaviour. It gives a confusing message and can suggest to children that hitting is acceptable. Although some people do smack, there are many more effective techniques that do not cause physical pain and do not leave the parents feeling guilty that they might have hurt their child. For those families who were brave enough to be honest about smacking their children, it was often a key reason for them asking for help.

Time out

So you've set the boundaries, stopped shouting and asked your child once nicely followed by once firmly, but he's still not doing as you ask. You can't ignore his behaviour, and you're feeling frustrated. This is the point when things can quickly escalate. You need to take tougher action and show clear authority while still staying in control.

Time out is exactly what the term suggests: time spent away from a difficult situation. It gives you a chance to calm down and remain in control if your child's behaviour is really beginning to get to you. It is also an extreme form of ignoring, and gives your child a clear consequence to his behaviour. Time out is a powerful tool if used correctly, but must be seen as a last resort after you've tried every other strategy. The only exception to this is when your child is aggressive, and there is no option for a second chance.

The principle of time out is that you put your child somewhere safe, boring and away from you for one minute for each year of his life, but not exceeding five minutes. Some of the *Little Angels* families had already tried time out, but either didn't make sure their child stayed put, or had shut him away for up to an hour. Once the child starts to play and forgets why he's been isolated, the technique loses its effectiveness.

RULES FOR TIME OUT

○ You can use time out after you have asked your child once nicely to do something, then once firmly, and are still being ignored.

○ If your child is aggressive, clearly state that it is unacceptable as soon as it happens: 'No, that is not nice. You must not punch your brother.'

○ With no further conversation, take your child to a safe and boring place for one minute for each year of his life (five minutes maximum).

○ You may need to carry your child if she is struggling or kicking out, but ignore this and do not speak to her, even if she hits or bites you. You don't need to show anger or aggression yourself.

○ You can take your child to:
  ● a bottom stair
  ● a chair in another room
  ● to another room where they are away from everyone

○ If you want to use the step or chair, you may at first need to teach your child that you expect him to stay there by holding him in a firm cuddle. You must look away from him and not speak or make eye contact until the time is up.

○ If you are unlikely to be able to hold your child without a fight, put her in a room away from you. It doesn't matter if it has to be her bedroom: it is only for a short time, and won't make a negative association with that room. But the more boring the room, the better.

○ Close the door or, if your child is likely to keep coming out, hold it shut for the allotted time. This is preferable to having to wrestle your child back into the room.

○ As you put your child in the room tell her, 'Time out now.' You can also briefly tell her that you will be holding the door so that she knows why she can't get out and that you will still be there.

○ Do not get into a conversation of any kind during the time out. Do not respond to your child at all, however much he tries to engage you. This is the most extreme form of ignoring, and as soon as you speak, you are giving your child attention again. If he rattles the door handle, hold tight. If he kicks the door, ignore it.

❍ When the time is up tell your child that she can come out. Briefly explain why she was put there and state that if she repeats the behaviour, she will be timed out again.

❍ If your child is still having a tantrum when the time out is over, ask him once nicely to stop, then once firmly. Explain briefly that he will go back into time out if he doesn't stop.

❍ If he continues to behave badly, repeat the time out for the same period of time.

❍ If your child comes out calmer, explain briefly why she went in, then have a cuddle and move on with your day.

❍ Do not mention the time out again, or hold a grudge. Praise and cuddle your child at the first opportunity after the time out in order for him to get a really clear message about his behaviour.

Some parents are resistant to the idea of using time out because they think it's cruel. It's worth remembering that if your child is crying when you put him into time out, it's more likely to be because he is cross with you for taking firm action. Remember, you're not hitting your child or screaming at him, and it's only ever for a short period.

Tracy Ellmore was herself in floods of tears the first time she put her three-year-old daughter India into time out in the bathroom. India's screams of indignation made Tracy feel guilty and sorry for her, but Tracy was surprised at how effective the time out was in giving India a clear message that she had to sit at the table and eat her dinner rather than charging around throwing food. Despite her reservations, she decided to persevere with the strategy, and quickly found that she barely had to use it on her triplets. As she realized, 'Now I don't shout or smack them. The threat of time out acts as a deterrent.'

It's also important not to overuse it. Lisa Williams had learnt to put Kieran on the bottom step for time out, but he was sent there so much and for so long that it had lost its power as a deterrent. In fact, it had simply become another venue for arguments, as Lisa would stand and row with Kieran while he was sitting on the step.

Time out also gave a very clear message to Nicola Georgiou, whose tantrums were both frequent and violent. Her mother Christina showed Nicola that she would no longer tolerate being hit by putting her in her bedroom for four minutes and holding the door shut. Christina initially found this upsetting, but was amazed at how quickly Nicola responded. Within a very short space of time the tantrums and hitting stopped, and Christina felt the cycle was breaking. 'I can feel myself being calm,' said Christina. 'I don't lose my temper.'

Nicola was also told that if she tried to force her mother to let her breastfeed, she would be put in time out. For the first time she got a

---

TIME OUT POINTS IN BRIEF

❍ Time = one minute for each year of your child's life (maximum five minutes).

❍ No chat or attention, just clear firm words and actions.

❍ Do not argue with your child at all.

❍ Make sure your child is somewhere safe.

❍ Put your child in a room if there would be a physical tussle on the step or chair.

❍ Hold the door shut if necessary, but let your child know you are there.

❍ Do not speak to him during the time out.

❍ Finish the time out with a clear explanation of why it occurred.

❍ Time out again if, after asking your child twice to behave, he continues to behave badly.

❍ When time out is over, move on with your day positively. Do not mention it or bear a grudge, and put all your effort into praising your child.

❍ Use loving, positive techniques that emphasize your child's better behaviour, enabling the tougher techniques to be more effective when you have to use them.

clear message from her mother that no really meant no. Just a warning that she would get time out was enough to stop her in her tracks. 'I felt I was in control,' reported Christina, 'as if to say I'm a changed mother.'

When not to use time out

Tamara Carrera was keen to learn strategies that would help her discipline Keanu, who could be very unruly and domineering, but time out would not have been a good technique for her to use. Keanu was already large for his age and physically dominant, so there was a good chance that trying to put him into time out would lead to a fight that might be hard to defuse. If you don't think you have the physical strength to put your child into time out, it's better not to use it. An alternative is to time yourself out by going into another room for a few minutes and shutting the door, but you need to make sure your child is safe before you do this.

It's also possible that time out, if given too quickly, can escalate a situation. Matthew Christie refused to help lay the table at dinner time, and instead tried to turn on the television. His father Brian asked him to sit down, but when Matthew refused, Brian quickly decided to put him into time out. Once upstairs, Matthew refused to come back down to dinner. It took his mother going upstairs and threatening him with another visit to the time out room before he would come down.

Although Matthew eventually ended up at the dinner table, there was a good chance Brian could have avoided the situation by ignoring Matthew until it was time to come and sit down, or by making laying the table into a game. It's always worth thinking through your options and being positive and creative in your approach before you jump in with a more hardline tactic.

POINTS TO REMEMBER

○ All children need clear boundaries in order to understand the rules around their behaviour. These should be decided upon and agreed by all involved in parenting your child.

○ Behaviour contracts between parents or between parents and older children can keep everyone clear and consistent about the family rules.

○ The response you give *immediately* after your child's behaviour has occurred will be extremely powerful in determining whether that behaviour is continued, maintained or reduced.

○ Once you have defined the boundaries around your children's behaviour, use your calm and consistent behaviour to show them where they stand.

○ In order to get your children to do as they are asked, you need to ask them once nicely, followed by once firmly. Make sure your voice and body language convey authority without shouting.

○ Actions speak louder than words. Do not negotiate or argue, especially with younger children, as your words are meaningless.

○ Use ignoring as much as you can for dealing with tantrums and difficult behaviour. You may need nerves of steel, but ignoring, combined with praise for lovely behaviour, will give children a powerful message.

○ Losing rewards and withdrawing privileges will show your children that their behaviour affects them as much as you. Always be calm and consistent when using sticker charts.

○ Time out is an extreme form of ignoring, which should be used when all else has failed, or the situation is spiralling out of control. Do not overuse this technique or it will lose its effectiveness. Try all other approaches first.

chapter five

Sweet
dreams

'YOU JUST GET THIS VICIOUS CIRCLE OF NO SLEEP, ARGUMENTS, FIGHTING, NO sleep… It's out of control and we've got to find some way to break it,' said Sam Norris. Anyone with a child who doesn't sleep will understand that feeling only too well. Sleep deprivation is a well-known form of torture. A broken night's sleep can lead to feeling fraught and irritable, and make getting through the next day an uphill struggle.

But tired as you may be, you're not alone. More than half the families who featured in *Little Angels* had children with a variety of sleep problems. Many parents were at the end of their tether, as exhaustion exacerbated their children's bad behaviour and put their relationships under terrible strain.

What's your problem?

Every child is unique, and every sleep problem has its own particular characteristics, but there are common features. You may well be able to recognize your problem in one or more of the following scenarios.

No bedtime routine: You may have a child like three-year-old Ayla Huseyin, who could never settle down enough to go to bed. Your child may be up all evening and into the early hours, unable to calm down and making demands.

Children can't fall asleep in their bed: Maybe, like the three-year-old Ellmore triplets, your child falls asleep anywhere but in his own bed: on the sofa, in your arms or even in your bed. You then carry him to his bed and creep out of the room, fearful that you will wake him.

Children won't stay in their bed: Perhaps your children, like five-year-old Luke Barton or the three-year-old Elson triplets, won't stay put in bed. They then disrupt your evening by coming downstairs or calling you upstairs with various requests, or they end up in your bed in the small hours, wriggling and keeping you awake.

Waking in the night: Your child, like three-year-old Katie Norris, may call out and cry constantly during the night, wanting drinks, cuddles or attention. You go in and out, hour after hour, and you're exhausted.

SAMPLE DAY OF A SLEEP DIARY (kept for Katie Norris)

Day	Morning waking times	Times of naps	Time in bed	What child did and what you did
Mon	06.30	14.30–15.30 in car	19.30	Gave juice, put on video, switched on the light – kept calling for more juice and video; Tim went in and did it.
Tue				
Wed				
Thu				
Fri				
Sat				
Sun				

Whatever the problem, if your life is disrupted by your child's night-time behaviour, you are probably desperate to change things. Poor sleep patterns usually develop because children haven't learnt to settle themselves to sleep in their own beds, or to sleep through the night in that same bed. Sometimes children may have health or neurological problems that affect their sleep patterns, but this is rare. The brutal truth is that most children who don't sleep well haven't been taught how to by their parents.

Keeping a sleep diary

As with other behaviour problems, change is possible, but you will need to adopt a positive attitude to managing the situation. You need to think first about how your own behaviour may have contributed to your child's sleep problem. Then you can patiently and consistently take control and help get your child into a routine that is better for all the family.

Time to sleep	Time(s) woken during the night	What you did/ time and place returned to sleep
22.25	1 23.05 2 01.30 3 02.45 4 03.20	Each time Tim went in with more juice and rewound video. Slept in own bed for rest of the night.

It will help to start off by keeping a diary (see pages 80–1) so that you can look at what your child is doing and at your responses. If your child has more than one nap during the day, note them all; if your child goes to bed and gets up several times, note and number each time this occurs. Do the same if there are multiple entries for the final two columns.

This diary should be kept as accurately as possible, which means that even when you are dealing with your child, bleary-eyed in the middle of the night, you must still try to record what happened and how she responded. It might be tough going, but you will need to fill in this diary for at least a week in order to have a really good understanding of the problem. As you read it back, consider the following questions:

1   Is there a routine before bed?
2   Do you decide when bedtime is and enforce it?
3   Does bedtime happen in a calm way, signalling that it is time to sleep?
4   Does your child fall asleep on his own and in his own bed?
5   Can your child fall asleep without any help, such as bottle or drink, television or light on?
6   Can you leave the bedroom before your child is asleep and leave her to fall asleep on her own?
7   Can your child settle himself to sleep without getting out of bed or calling for you?
8   Can your child sleep through the night in her bed on her own?
9   If your child calls out in the night, can you comfort him briefly, then leave him to go back to sleep?
10 Can you and your partner enjoy your bed as your own without extra bedmates during the night?

If you have answered no to most or all of the above, you need to read on and learn new ways to manage your child's sleep.

Understanding the problem

Of course, all parents want their children to sleep, but in our desire for peace we can sometimes create worse problems. By recording footage shot at night, we were able to reveal to the *Little Angels* families how they were mismanaging their children's sleep. Lack of sleep was often having a knock-on effect to daytime behaviour.

For Jane and Barry Soilleux, their moment of truth came when they watched footage of three-year-old Emily's constant whinging. In one scene Emily was out shopping with her mother and whining, 'I want my daddy, I want my milk.' What Jane and Barry hadn't realized was that this was 'code' for 'I'm exhausted and I want to go to sleep'. The reason for this was that Emily's bedtime routine consisted of drinking a bottle of milk and falling asleep on the sofa next to her dad after her siblings and mother had gone to bed. In Emily's mind, sleep meant Daddy, milk, sofa and TV.

Barry and Jane had had good intentions in allowing this routine, the idea being to prevent Emily's playing up disturbing her older brother and sister, who were at school. Emily was kept downstairs to fall asleep, and put into her own bed later, but it meant that she was falling asleep very late and not getting enough hours' sleep for her age. Barry and Jane were unaware that she was getting three hours' less sleep a night than she needed, and was extremely sleep-deprived. To resolve her constant whinging and temper tantrums, they first had to sort out her poor sleep pattern.

It was also a revelation for Nigel and Bianca Price that three-year-old Ella's tantrums and biting, five-year-old Herbie's defiance and seven-year-old Miles's poor concentration were a direct result of sleep deprivation. None of their children had a clear bedtime routine. They roamed around the flat all evening and watched TV in their shared room until they eventually fell asleep at around 10.30 p.m. Nigel and Bianca were surprised to learn that before they could sort out any behaviour problems, they had to teach their children to get a good night's sleep. They were also shocked to hear that Ella needed to be in bed by 7 p.m., and Herbie by 7.30 or 8 p.m. They simply hadn't realized how much sleep children of those ages needed.

What is normal?

If your child isn't getting enough sleep, this may be leading to other problems with her behaviour. Below is a chart that outlines the average amount of sleep your child needs at different ages. Of course, children are all individuals, so there will be differences, but if you are finding that your child is getting much less than the recommended amount, you need to take action. You should also check that she is not having too much of the recommended amount as naps during the day rather than during night hours.

AVERAGE SLEEP REQUIREMENTS

Age	Total sleep (hours)	Night sleep (hours)	Naps (number of times)
6 months	$14^{1/4}$	11	2
9 months	14	$11^{1/2}$	2
12 months	$13^{3/4}$	$11^{1/2}$	2
18 months	$13^{1/2}$	$11^{1/2}$	1
2 years	13	$11^{1/2}$	1
3 years	12	11	1
4 years	$11^{1/2}$		
5 years	11		
6 years	$10^{3/4}$		
9 years	10		

Between the ages of six and 12 months children should be settled in a regular sleep pattern, getting the appropriate number of hours' sleep per night and in daytime naps. They should have a clear bedtime routine, be able to go down in their cot or bed, and fall asleep on their own. They should also be able to sleep through most nights. Some parents are very lucky in having babies who fall into a routine on their own very early; others are less lucky, and have to shape their child's behaviour by teaching good sleep habits. If you think you fit the latter description, you need to find ways of helping your child (and yourself) to sleep again.

Getting positive

Some children find that playing up at bedtime is a good way of getting attention. Kathy Cooper's sons Jay and Owen weren't getting enough positive interaction during the day, so they had learnt to make up for that by causing havoc at night. Bouncing in and out of bed and trying to get their mother to go upstairs turned into a game for them. It was guaranteed to wind Kathy up, while the boys got lots of attention for doing it.

If your child is not only behaving badly during the day but also keeping you up at night, you may well have a negative attitude towards him. Lisa Williams was at the end of her tether with four-year-old Kieran, and the frustration continued long into the night. 'I think I'd describe bedtime as him having one last go at winding me up,' she said.

If you feel like this, it's worth remembering that you will need to feel positive about your child and your ability to manage her before you attempt to tackle her sleep problems. This is understandably difficult, especially if you are sleep-deprived and finding life tough going; but it's vital if you are to make calm and confident changes.

A positive step is to recognize the difference between a 'bad' child and one who is behaving badly because he is exhausted. If, in your mind, the bad child is responsible for his behaviour and not very likeable, your attitude is likely to be a negative one. An exhausted child behaving badly is far more likely to be lovely once he is getting enough sleep.

Setting a bedtime routine

For Sam and Tim Norris, bedtimes were chaotic. Although two-year-old Amy and three-year-old Katie were usually put to bed on time, Sam and Tim had developed a complex system of getting the girls to settle, which included beakers of juice, a video playing and the overhead light on. This system had evolved as a way of avoiding Katie having tantrums at bedtime, but it now meant that Tim was called into the bedroom for beaker refills and video rewinds up to six times a night. He and Sam never got an evening to themselves, and had barely slept a night through in three years.

For Katie, sleep meant TV, light, beaker and Daddy. She had built a psychological dependence on having these props to help her sleep, so if her beaker was empty or the video stopped, she needed her dad to come in throughout the night and provide them for her again. It is quite normal to wake very briefly at times during the night, but we are usually unaware of this and will fall back to sleep. However, if your child, like Katie, is dependent on external props to help him get back to sleep, he will call for you or come to find you when he wakes up. Katie needed a new routine, which meant 'unlearning' what she was used to and learning one that would help her get herself off to sleep unaided in a darkened room.

Many of the parents in the TV series were making the most funda-mental mistake when it came to helping their children learn good sleep patterns. They were not setting up sleep by providing a consistently calm and relaxing routine that signalled to their children that it was time to go to bed and fall asleep.

Ideal bedtime routine
○ Teatime.
○ Playtime/watching TV.
○ Bathtime – calm but fun.
○ Into night clothes.
○ Final drink (ideally milk rather than juice, which is sugary) as stories are read, preferably in the bedroom, with low lighting and a calm atmosphere.

○ Warn your child when it is the last story.
○ Close the book and say, 'It's night time, it's time to go to sleep.'
○ Clean teeth.
○ Remain calm and do not engage in any conversation or arguments.
○ Kiss and cuddle.
○ Turn out the light and leave, taking the beaker/cup with you.
○ Bedroom is in darkness or with a night-light, but no TV or music on. The presence of light can disrupt the body clock.

Finally, your child needs a loving and secure environment to drop off to sleep happily, safe in the knowledge that you'll be there in the morning. If you've been fighting with your child during the day, now is not the time to continue your row. Kieran and Lisa Williams were in so much conflict that continued bedtime arguments were making him anxious and more likely to play up. Melissa Christoforou got so annoyed with her eight-year-old daughter Indianna about going to bed that she found it hard to make up and hug her, which made Indianna even more demanding of her mother's affection. However annoying your child has been, bedtime needs to be loving and calm.

TOP BEDTIME TIPS
○ Baths are a useful way of relaxing children. Increasing the body's core temperature can help induce sleep.
○ Playtime and television should happen only before baths, as once night clothes are on, activity has to decrease and the atmosphere become calm, again signalling to your child that bedtime is approaching.
○ Do not allow your children drinks, TV or any other 'props' to help them get to sleep (such as being rocked in your arms), as you will be forever running in and out to provide more. If your children sleep with the light on and turning it off suddenly might scare them, get a night-light. If you think they can't go to bed without milk, reduce the amount you give them each night, or dilute it with water over time until they lose interest in drinking it.

Getting to bed – and staying there

Once your child is calm and ready for bed, the challenge is to get him into it and ensure he stays there.

On *Little Angels* we suggested four main approaches to deal with children who wouldn't stay in bed.

1 Gradual withdrawal
2 Rapid return
3 Door shutting
4 Sticker charts and incentives

The approach you take depends to some extent on what kind of child you have and how entrenched your problem is. It also depends on how comfortable you feel about leaving your child and using the rapid-return method or the door-shutting technique. If you are not comfortable with these, you might prefer the gentler approaches of gradual withdrawal or using a sticker chart. Whatever you decide to do, remember to remain positive that your child will learn to stay in bed.

1 Gradual withdrawal

Katie

Tim and Sam were anxious that putting Katie to bed without her drink, TV or light on would make her scream and disturb her sister. The TV was removed from the bedroom and a night-light put in. After a new, calm evening routine of bath, milk and story, Tim put Katie into bed and sat on the end of it until she seemed relaxed and settled, which was reassuring for both of them. While he sat on the bed, he looked away and had no contact with her. If she sat up, Tim had to gently but firmly lay her back down without any conversation, except to say very quietly, 'It's time to go to sleep'. Katie settled very quickly, and Tim left the room as she was falling asleep. Both parents were surprised at how easy it had been.

Katie had been used to calling out for her father during the night, so there was a good chance that she would continue to do this for the first few nights of her new routine. It was planned that if she did, Tim would go in and sit near her, but not interact with her, until she settled and began falling asleep. This would be to reassure her that she had not been suddenly abandoned, as she was so used to seeing Tim during the night. In the event, Tim did not need to do this because Katie slept through the night from the first day of her new routine. Her parents were shocked and thrilled. 'It's been years since we've had a good night's sleep with the children in the house,' said Sam.

Emily

Three-year-old Emily had got used to going to sleep on the sofa while drinking a bottle of milk with her father. These were her cues for going to sleep. It was important to help her 'unlearn' these and replace them with learning to fall asleep alone in her own bed.

Her parents, Jane and Barry, felt that it would be too brutal just to put her into bed and leave her because it would be so unfamiliar and might cause her to wake her brother and sister, with whom she shared a room. So to help her slowly reduce her dependency on Daddy, sofa and bottle, they were gradually withdrawn.

Barry (whom she associated with sleep) had to put Emily into bed and lie next to her until she fell asleep. Jane and Barry also swapped the bedtime bottle for a beaker of milk, and slowly reduced the amount in it each night. Once Emily was able to settle herself to sleep alone in her own bed, she was told that the beaker of milk could not go into the bedroom any more and had to be finished downstairs.

Barry was told that he was to lie with Emily for the first few nights, then, as she got more used to her bed, he could sit near her for a few nights. Then he moved to the end of the bed for a few nights, then sat by the door, and then, when she seemed able to settle herself, he was able leave the room and stand outside until he was sure she was asleep. In this way he was weaning Emily off her dependence on him. If Emily tried to engage him in conversation of any kind, he was to lay her down firmly, telling her it was time to go to sleep, and then look away.

At first Barry found the process hard, especially as he tended to fall asleep on Emily's bed while all three children played around him. But his perseverance paid off, and within two weeks Emily was falling asleep in her own bed. Emily protested for a couple of nights about not having her bottle, but Barry sat with her again as she settled herself off to sleep and she got used to it.

As Emily began to get more sleep, her behaviour started improving. Barry and Jane were delighted. 'It was so obvious, and yet we couldn't see it at the time,' said Jane. 'You just think, why did I do that?' There was a bonus for their relationship too. 'We never got any time together to talk because Emily was always there,' said Jane. 'I actually feel like I'm married now.'

2 Rapid return
Herbie, Miles and Ella

The Price children were also given a new bath and story routine before being put to bed much earlier than usual. The TV had been removed from their room. On the first night Miles, the eldest, seemed to settle straight away, but five-year-old Herbie immediately got out of bed, pro-duced a gun and sunglasses from the toy-box and headed for the door. His father Nigel was told to take him firmly but gently back to his bed with no chat or fuss. All he should say was, 'It's night time. It's time to go to sleep,' then leave the room. Herbie reappeared sobbing, and again was gently taken back to bed.

It's important not to get drawn in if your child cries, as he is very likely to do when he realizes that you mean business. Keep your manner matter of fact. If your child becomes very distressed when you start your new approach, it might be because the change in the environment is too abrupt. Herbie was used to falling asleep with the noise and light from a television, so a silent, dark bedroom made him feel anxious. Nigel therefore left the door ajar and sat on the end of Herbie's bed for a few minutes. This was to help wean him off his dependency on the TV, while still ensuring that he stayed in bed.

Within a few minutes, Herbie had settled, and the rapid-return technique worked on subsequent evenings. Within a short space of time, all three children were regularly getting two to three hours' more sleep a night, and their behaviour improved dramatically. Miles had the added bonus of doing better at school. 'I feel a bit stupid for not having done it before,' Bianca said, but she simply hadn't realized how much a lack of sleep was contributing to her children's behaviour.

Ayla

Three-year-old Ayla Huseyin hated going to bed. She had no real bedtime routine and had never slept through a single night in her own bed. She usually fell asleep in her parents' bed at around midnight, then Alev or Somer would carry her into her own bed later. When she woke in the night she would return to her parents' bed and either stay there until morning, or be repeatedly returned to her own bed. 'I haven't had a decent night's sleep in three years,' grumbled Somer.

Unsurprisingly, this routine was leaving Ayla sleep-deprived and very badly behaved during the day. When Alev and Somer started filming with *Little Angels* they were at breaking point, especially as their third child was due in just one month's time.

It was important for Alev and Somer to start with a calmer bedtime routine. Ayla was often highly excitable and active during the evenings. In one scene Somer was seen vigorously play-fighting with her in a bid, he said, to 'knacker her out'. This was having the opposite effect, and making her more excited. Instead, Alev gave Ayla a calm bubble bath and read to her over milk. A night-light was put in her room. The plan was then to try the gradual withdrawal method.

But as soon as Ayla realized that she was going to be put to bed, she began to have a tantrum. First Alev, then Somer, tried to lie beside her while she lashed out, hitting and biting them. It became clear that the approach for Ayla had to be all or nothing, so they switched to using the rapid-return technique.

Somer was told to leave the room where Ayla was in bed. He then stood outside, and every time she got out of bed and came to the door, he would gently but firmly carry her back into bed, saying, 'It's night time, go to sleep,' in a calm and boring voice. He would then leave the room and repeat the process if she got up again. Ayla had to be put back into bed a total of 26 times, but Somer kept going, and she eventually gave in, exhausted. Her parents had shown her that they were in control, and that night, for the first time ever, Ayla slept through in her own bed. Somer was ecstatic. 'I was in heaven,' he said. 'I've never had such a restful sleep.'

The next few nights were tough going, with many rapid return trips to bed. Spurred on by the thought of the new baby arriving, Alev and Somer were determined not to give in. Within four nights, Ayla was sleeping in her own bed. Even when her sleep pattern was disrupted by the arrival of her baby sister Tulay, Alev and Somer used the rapid-return method again, and got her back on track within a couple of nights.

Luke and Elliot

Bedtime in the Barton household was a battlefield. 'They create any excuse to stay up and come downstairs,' said mum Jo of five-year-old Luke and three-year-old Elliot. 'That's if I get them upstairs in the first place. And when they do get upstairs there'll be tears for something else.' The boys would be up and down all evening, and it would often be 10 p.m. before they were asleep, leaving Jo to grab a bowl of cereal before collapsing in front of the TV. 'It would be nice to have a bit of time in the evening when we can sit and eat dinner,' Jo reflected.

The first step was to tighten up the bedtime routine so that the boys would not come downstairs and watch TV after their bath. Their younger brother Harrison was put to bed first, then Jo read Elliot a calm story. He went off to bed without a hitch. But older brother Luke didn't want to go to bed, and tried to run away. His father Jason had to catch him calmly, without making it into a game, and put him into bed with as little chat as possible. Luke was protesting that he didn't want to go to bed, but Jason just had to keep blandly repeating, 'It's night time, it's time to go to sleep.'

Every time Luke got out of bed he was calmly picked up and taken back. If he called out but was still in his bed, his parents had to ignore his calls. It seemed that Luke had settled, until he was spotted sitting at the top of the stairs looking grumpy. Despite feeling sorry for his son and wanting to give him a cuddle, Jason remained firm and took him back to bed with no conversation. Luke soon fell asleep, having learnt an important lesson: that bedtime antics would no longer get any attention.

That night Jo and Jason were astonished to find themselves 'boy-free at 8 o'clock'. They continued to use rapid return and tried to ignore any of the boys' bids for attention. 'We've now got Luke and Elliot up into bed earlier, with a lot less fuss, which means we have more free time in the evening and a better night. And it's excellent!' said Jason.

3 Shutting the door

Jessica

'She gets up virtually every night and she'll scream the house down until we fetch her out of the bedroom,' said Mick Butler of his five-year-old daughter Jessica. Mick and his wife Claire had got so desperate to get Jessica to sleep that the more she cried, the more they gave in to her, letting her go up and downstairs, lie on the sofa and watch videos in her room. 'We've made bed a bad place to go,' admitted Claire. 'It highlights our desperation for her just to sleep; regardless of whether it's in the fast lane of the M6, we just want her to go to sleep!'

As Jessica had become so powerful and was very strong-willed, Mick and Claire were taught to use an alternative to rapid return. After a calming bedtime routine, Jessica was put to bed. She started crying the moment she was put into her bed, but was told that if she got up, her bedroom door would be closed. If she stayed in bed, however, she could have it open. She immediately jumped out of bed and Claire held the door shut for one minute, telling Jessica through the door that she needed to get back into bed. Jessica stood by the door screaming and trying to yank it open, but Claire had to stand firm.

When the minute was up Claire opened the door and told Jessica that if she wanted to keep it open, she needed to be in bed. The idea was to teach Jessica that she was the one who could control whether the door was open, by staying in bed. Each time the door was held shut for slightly longer, to a maximum of five minutes. It was a steep learning curve for Jessica, and she put up a fierce fight. Over a period of nearly two hours Claire had to open and shut the door 24 times before Jessica got into bed and fell asleep.

The following night Jessica put up another spirited battle, and cried until she was sick. But Claire and Mick calmly cleared it up and kept going. Within a week, Jessica was going to bed without a struggle, and the difference in her behaviour was marked. 'Everybody has seen the difference in Jessica since she started to sleep,' said Mick. Claire agreed: 'She's lost the grumpiness that was always apparent in her.'

Rio, India and Carlo

Tracy Ellmore's three-year-old triplets Rio, India and Carlo were often still awake at 11 p.m. Tracy would struggle to get them settled in front of the TV, then carry them up to bed after they had dropped off. One by one they would wake during the night and go into Tracy's bed, where they all spent a fitful night. The triplets' behaviour during the day was very unruly, and Tracy was worried that they would be unable to cope when they started nursery in just a few weeks' time.

As Tracy is a single mum and has to manage three children at once, the best approach to improving their sleep habits was to try the door-shutting technique. The triplets reacted with surprise the first time the bedroom door was shut, and it took Rio, India and Carlo over an hour to give up and settle in their own beds. But after only two nights they were getting the message that if they got out of bed, the door would be closed. Within a very short space of time the triplets were sleeping from 7.30 p.m. to 7 a.m. 'I don't even have to shut the door now,' said Tracy. 'I just have to threaten it and they get back in bed and lie down.' Tracy was delighted with the freedom and rest that the new routine brought her. 'There's no going back now,' she insisted.

4 Using sticker charts and incentives

Romany, Bayley and Velvet

Matt and Mandie Elson have five children, with three-year-old triplets Bayley, Romany and Velvet sharing a room. Bedtime for the triplets was often noisy and unruly, with them frequently getting out of bed. Matt and Mandie would be constantly in and out of their room answering requests, so the triplets got a lot of attention for messing around. Sometimes they would be put back to bed, sometimes shouted at, and sometimes left to stay up for a while by their exhausted parents, who did not have the energy for a struggle.

VELVET'S SLEEP CHART

	Mon	Tues	Weds	Thurs	Fri	Sat	Sun
Stay in bed	✗	☺	☺	☺	☺	☺	☺
Go straight to sleep	✗	☺	✗	☺	✗	☺	☺

Matt and Mandie were asked to follow a new and calmer bedtime routine, where chaos and noise were replaced by a relaxing bath and stories in bed. When they left the room they were told to ignore all calling out and to use the rapid-return technique if one of the triplets left the room. On the first night the girls had to be put back 20 times, while Bayley stayed in bed.

Before bed, the triplets were each given their own simple sticker chart and were told that they would get one smiley sticker for staying in bed, and another for going straight to sleep. Two stickers in the morning meant a small treat.

On the first morning Velvet and Romany had not earned their treats; when they had to watch their brother Bayley get his they were both very upset. The impact of this can be seen on the second night, when Velvet appeared to learn and got her treat. On night three she pushed the boundaries and lost out, but was back on track by night four, and after a wobble on night five, had learnt to stay in her bed and go to sleep. Mandie found it difficult to see her daughters upset at losing their treats, but she and Matt persevered. Soon the spirit of competition among the triplets, plus Matt and Mandie's consistent behaviour at bedtime, meant that nights in the Elson house were much calmer.

Ayla, Katie, Emily

Other children who were poor sleepers were offered incentives to stay in bed. When going to bed for the first time with a night-light in their rooms, Katie and Ayla were both told that the Night-light Fairy would be watching how good they were. If they went to sleep in their beds and stayed there, they would get a small treat from her in the morning. Both were thrilled with their gifts when they awoke. When Emily had her last bottle she was told that if she left it out, the Bottle Fairy would leave her a big girl's beaker to replace it, with a little treat inside.

Be creative in your handling of sleep problems. Little children love magic, and the thought of a fairy coming to see them sleep and leave them a treat is as powerful as the threat of Father Christmas not leaving their toys if they are still awake on Christmas Eve.

Don't worry that your child will become used to having a treat every morning for sleeping and that you will soon become bankrupt. All the poor sleepers on *Little Angels* soon forgot about the treat, in the same way that children lose interest in sticker charts once their behaviour has improved. You can also wean them off the treat by increasing the number of nights they have to sleep in order to get it.

Finally, do not use food as a treat. A football card or a small glittery pencil are all it takes, plus the most important treat – your praise and affection.

Getting through the night

Having got their children into bed, some of the *Little Angels* families had successfully resolved their children's sleep problems. However, some families still had a little further to go, as their children would wake in the night and either call out for their parents or go and get into their bed.

However hard it sounds, the broad rule is that if you don't want your children in your bed, you will only discourage them by taking them straight back to their own bed whenever they get into yours. Every time you roll over and go back to sleep with your children snuggled along-side, you are reinforcing their idea that it is all right to do so.

Three-year-old Ayla was very skilled at getting into her parents' bed at night without them realizing it. This had come about because they were so exhausted by broken nights, but not stopping it simply gave her permission to continue the behaviour. As they were soon to have a newborn baby in their room, it was even more urgent for them to make sure Ayla stayed in her own bed all night. One problem was that Ayla needed milk and a dummy to go to sleep; if she woke in the night and one of them was missing, she would call out or go into her parents' bed. This was their new approach:

○ They put chimes on their door handle so that they would wake up when Ayla came in and prevent her getting into their bed.

○ Taking it in turns each night, they would take her straight back to her bed with no fuss or chat, no cuddles or attention.

○ If she kept coming out, they would use the same rapid-return technique as they did at her bedtime – calmly and firmly returning her to her bed.

○ They tied her dummy to a very short length of ribbon, which they pinned to the side of her mattress so that she could reach down and get it. (Although they wanted her off the dummy, there were so many changes to make that it was the last thing to go.)

○ They watered down her milk each night until she lost interest in having it with her in bed.

Other problems
Siblings

You might be worried that your child will wake the sibling she shares a room with while you are trying to make changes to her sleep behaviour. Often this doesn't happen if the sibling is already in a deep sleep. Amy Norris, for example, slept through her sister Katie being put to bed. Sometimes the sibling may be awake, but stays in bed and eventually falls asleep, even with the commotion going on, as did Miles Price while his brother was being returned to bed by his father. On occasion, a very noisy and protesting child might wake a sibling: Ayla woke her 18-month-old sister Esin on the first night of her new sleep routine. If this happens, take the sibling out of the room and put her into your bed to sleep while you persevere with the sleep programme.

If you have children of very different ages, they should have different bedtimes. Ivan and Sue Angell were putting nine-year-old Bethany to bed at the same time as her three-year-old sister, and Bethany was then reading under the bedclothes. It's better to give older children some time with you uninterrupted by their younger siblings. If you have an older child and a younger child sharing a bedroom, it also helps to separate their spaces so that the older child feels she has some privacy. Melissa Christoforou was worried that eight-year-old Indianna was disturbing three-year-old Violet, so she separated their bunk beds and made Indianna her own corner of the room.

Night feeding

If you have a child like Ayla who wakes in the night for drinks, you can try the following techniques:

❍ Stop the drinks immediately.
❍ Reduce the amount of milk in the beaker each night.
❍ Dilute the drink with increasing amounts of water each night.

Again, choose what you think will work best for your child.

Early waking

If your children are early risers, you can use a sticker chart as a means of rewarding them for not coming to you straight away and instead playing quietly in their room. You can also get clocks that show children when it is a reasonable hour for them to wake others.

If your children are still having naps, consider whether they are sleeping too much in the day. If you calculate from your diary that your children are already getting the required amount of sleep, it might be sensible to put them to bed slightly later, with the aim of pushing their wake-up time to later in the morning.

Letting your child cry

Leaving your child to cry is sometimes known as 'controlled crying', and many parents find it an upsetting technique. It is important to decide whether your child's crying is genuine distress, or comes more from frustration and rage. If your child is distressed by the new approach to bedtime, use a gradual approach, as described for Emily (see page 89). If your child is in a rage like Ayla, who was kicking and biting, the all-or-nothing approach probably works better (see page 91). Remember, as soon as you give in and enter the bedroom to pick up, cuddle or talk to your child, you are back to square one because you have given attention to the behaviour you don't want.

If you choose to leave your child crying, you can go in at intervals and briefly show him that you are there, tell him quietly that it is night time and time to go to sleep, then leave. Be boring and calm, and increase the amount of time between checking. Make sure the moment your child falls asleep is a moment when you are not in the room. Do not keep checking once he is quiet, as he might be settling himself and your appearance will only disrupt things again.

If, like Herbie Price or Jessica Butler, your child can cry so much that she is sick, you need to remember that if you give her lots of attention, it can increase the chances of it happening again. Your approach should be calm and firm. Quickly change your child's clothes and sheets with no attention, conversation or cuddles. Remember, if you don't want a behaviour to occur, the quickest way to get rid of it is to ignore it as much as you can.

Making bedtime earlier

If you are intending to use one of the approaches we have described with children who go to bed very late, do not set yourself up to fail by initially putting them to bed a lot earlier. It's best to start around the bedtime they are used to, then cut it back by 10 minutes each night until they get to a good bedtime. You can work out what this should be by using the sleep requirements chart (see page 84) and working backwards from when your children usually wake up.

If you have older children who are protesting about going to bed, you can involve them in negotiating an appropriate bedtime. Melissa Christoforou did this with Indianna, bargaining her down from the extra hour she wanted to just 15 minutes. This time was then spent together quietly, helping to strengthen their relationship, which had become very fraught.

POINTS TO REMEMBER

❍ If your child has a sleep problem, it could be due to one or more of the following:

- He has no bedtime routine.
- She can't fall asleep in her own bed.
- He won't stay in his own bed.
- She wakes in the night.

❍ Your child's sleep, like his behaviour will be influenced by your responses. If you give attention to sleep problems, they will continue.

❍ Sleep is an important part of your child's development, and if she does not get enough, she is likely to develop problems with her behaviour, attention and concentration. Does your child get adequate amounts of sleep for her age?

❍ Keep a diary so that you can understand the kind of problem your child has, and how you are reinforcing and maintaining it.

❍ Recognize that you have given your child control over his sleep pattern and that you must start to take it back in order to help him learn healthier sleep behaviour.

❍ Calm, consistent and relaxing bedtime routines are a vital first step in solving sleep difficulties.

❍ Your child needs to 'unlearn' her inappropriate sleep associations, such as falling asleep on the sofa or in front of the TV, or sucking on a bottle. She will need help to learn appropriate new associations, which include:

- Falling asleep in her room.
- Falling asleep in her own bed.
- Falling asleep in the dark or semi-darkness.
- Having no other noise or distractions, such as the TV.
- Not drinking.
- Being alone.

○ You can adopt strategies where you gradually teach your child the new sleep behaviour by slowly withdrawing his dependence on the props that help him fall asleep. Alternatively, you can adopt an instant all-or-nothing approach.

○ If your child cries in the night and you go in to comfort her or give her drinks, she will continue to call out in the night. All responses must be given with the minimum of fuss and attention. No attention for the problem behaviour ➤ no more of the problem behaviour.

○ If you are tackling a number of problems, give yourself a chance to succeed by taking them one at a time. Establish a good bedtime routine before you tackle the night waking. Each bit of learning will help towards resolving the other problem behaviour.

○ Be realistic in your approach. Always:

• Set achievable goals, e.g. if your child currently goes to bed at 10 p.m., don't start trying to put him to bed at 7.30 p.m.

• Remain calm and consistent in your approach.

• Be boring and ignore your child if you need to go and sit by him as he learns to sleep in his own bed.

• Keep a diary of your progress. When you are tired you may not notice small changes each night, so you might become disheartened and give up if you don't keep a record. If you have to return your child to bed 37 times the first night, but only 19 times the next night, that's progress!

• Remember that children sometimes get worse when presented with new rules and boundaries before they get better. Remain positive and stay consistent and firm in your approach.

○ Change takes time, but the more consistent you are in your new behaviour towards your child, the faster he will learn and the sooner everyone in your household will be having sweet dreams.

chapter six

Eat up!

ANY PARENT WHO HAS SLAVED OVER THE COOKER TO MAKE THEIR CHILDREN A TASTY, nutritious meal will know how frustrating it can be when they then refuse to eat it. Feeding and parenting go hand in hand, and meals form the backbone of every day spent caring for children. Yet the table can often be a key battleground because children can exert power here, as much as they can in other areas. Short of force-feeding them, you can't make them eat.

Food lies at the very heart of parenting. Ensuring our children get enough to eat is one of our most basic and primitive instincts. For all parents the first anxiety they will have to deal with after the birth of a child is how, when and how much to feed him. Early feeding experiences can have a profound effect both on your children's relationship with food and how you deal with the continuing job of feeding them as they grow older.

What's the problem?

For many parents mealtimes can be a battleground with their children, who may:

❍ Refuse to eat.
❍ Not eat enough.
❍ Be very fussy and demanding about what they eat.
❍ Behave badly at the table.

On *Little Angels* we met several families whose relationships were coloured by eating and mealtime difficulties. We met children who had problems with food and eating, as well children who behaved badly at mealtimes. The parents had often got locked into a cycle of negative interaction with them, which could be both aggressive and anxious. As with other types of behaviour, the way children behave around food can be affected by those most closely involved in feeding them. If your children have poor eating habits, it is most likely to be because of the way you have taught them to eat.

You may be worried that your child isn't eating enough, or eating a broad enough range of foods. You may be fighting with him over sitting at table, or he may be throwing food around. The key to understanding your child's problem behaviour is to look at your own. Are you giving the right message around mealtimes, or are you reinforcing the bad behaviour by giving it lots of attention? Ask yourself the following questions:

○ Does your child have a regular mealtime pattern?
○ Does she eat at a table or, if the appropriate age, sit in a high chair?
○ Does she sit well and focus on her eating?
○ Does she stay seated in the high chair or at the table until she has finished eating?
○ Does she feed herself if she is able to?
○ Do you find feeding your child a pleasurable experience?

If you have answered no to these questions, you need to start monitoring your own and your child's behaviour at mealtimes. In addition, ask yourself the following questions:

○ Do you stand over or sit by your child and watch him eat?
○ Do you spend a lot of the meal commenting on his eating?
○ Do you nag him about his eating?
○ Do you try to bribe your child to eat?
○ If your child refuses to eat certain foods, do you often automatically get other foods for him?
○ Do mealtimes take more than 15 minutes?
○ Does your child open the fridge or cupboards and help himself to

what he wants when he wants, including at mealtimes?

○ Does your child eat most of his meals in front of the TV?

○ Do you wipe your child's hands and mouth more than once before he has finished eating?

If you have answered yes to some of these questions, you can begin to see why your child's eating is such a problem for you both. It's time to start monitoring the situation by keeping a simple diary for a minimum of one week. (See the example overleaf, which shows a typical day with three-year-old Elodie, one of Zora Lunniss's identical twin girls.)

When you look at your diary, first try to work out whether your child is behaving badly or has a specific problem with feeding. It may be a combination of both, but try to decide which is the main problem. This will influence the action you take.

What does the behaviour mean?

Zora's main worry was that her twin girls weren't getting a broad enough diet and were refusing to eat fruit and vegetables. 'I want them to have a much more varied diet,' she said. 'I want to be able to cook the meals and for them to eat them. They don't have to eat all of it, just some of it.' The twins would carefully pick any vegetables she offered them off their plates, and would often lay down the law about which bowl they were going to eat out of, what shape the food was cut in and how the ketchup should be poured.

Looking at Zora's food diary for Elodie (Asha's was very similar), it was clear that the twins were not eating an adequate range of foods for healthy development. They were eating too many sugary snacks between meals, and very little of the nutritious food they needed at mealtimes. They were also filling up on milk and yoghurts. Parents often complain that their child eats 'nothing', but on examination it turns out that the child is 'grazing' throughout the day. Not eating meals and filling up in between on drinks and snacks, especially milk and juice, can leave children less hungry at mealtimes, and therefore less likely to eat.

SAMPLE DAY OF A FEEDING DIARY (kept for Elodie Lunniss)

Date/ Time	Meal or snack	What you gave and how much	What your child ate and where
Mon, 15/11 07.45	Breakfast	Bowl of Coco Pops	4 spoonfuls Kitchen worktop
08.20	Snack	2 small packets biscuits	All In front of TV
11.35	Snack	Quavers	As above
12.25	Lunch	Spag bol, broccoli, yoghurt, juice	5 spoonfuls spag bol, 2 yoghurts Kitchen: table, worktop, my lap
13.10	Snack	Sweets, Fruit Shoot	All In buggy
15.00	Snack	Crisps	All In front of TV
16.45	Snack	1 slice bread & jam	As above
17.20	Supper	Chicken, rice & peas, banana, juice, yoghurt.	9 spoonfuls. No peas. Half banana, 2 yoghurts In kitchen – all over the place
19.45 (bedtime)	Snacks	Milk, crisps & biscuits	All In front of TV

Length of meal	What your child did	What you did
20 mins	Wanted bowl changed, then amounts in bowl changed.	Shouted, argued. Changed bowls. Changed amounts. Threw bowl in sink and walked out.
5 mins	Tantrum for biscuits for 15 mins.	Gave in. Shouted.
As above		
25 mins	Took out broccoli. Very cross. Picked out veg in spag bol. Helped herself to yoghurts from the fridge.	Shouted. Pleaded. Discussed. Bribed. Gave up. Nightmare.
Less than a minute!	Screaming in buggy.	Gave sweets to shut her up.
Fast	Demanded them	Too tired to say no. Want day to end.
Fast	Said was hungry. Enjoyed it.	At least she's eating, but worried about supper.
25 mins	Some fuss about the peas. Took ages to eat, fighting with her sister.	Pleaded with her to eat. Got cross. Tried to ignore. Shouted and threw food away. Tired & grumpy.
		On my knees.

But it wasn't just the twins' diet that was a problem. Zora was also locked in a battle of wills with the girls, which clouded all aspects of their life together. The kitchen was the main arena for their fights, and Zora's diary shows that she was playing a part in the twins' eating problems.

❍ She had given them control of their eating habits.

❍ She was giving most attention to their poor eating habits and bad behaviour at mealtimes, and was thus reinforcing the problem.

As the twins wouldn't eat what they were given, Zora was trapped in a vicious cycle. She would shout when they wouldn't eat, which would lead to the twins having tantrums and Zora giving in. This would make it more likely that they would refuse the same food when offered it again.

In addition to this, Zora was making some fundamental feeding mistakes:

❍ The children ate food in a variety of places and often in front of the TV.

❍ They had control of the cupboards and the fridge.

❍ Zora gave in to the twins' demands for snacks, so they were less likely to eat meals.

❍ Mealtimes took too long.

❍ Zora showed her girls how anxious she was about mealtimes.

SNACKS

❍ Small snacks can be offered between meals, but need to be well before the next meal.

❍ Snacks may offer good opportunities to introduce new foods. Children may refuse a particular food at mealtime, but accept it for a snack.

❍ Ideal snacks are fresh fruit, dried fruit or plain biscuits. It's best to steer clear of salty snacks, such as crisps, and sweets or chocolate.

❍ Do not allow your children to graze throughout the day on snack-type foods or they may not eat their main meals.

Feeling anxious

Like Zora, many parents with children who are poor eaters have anxiety at the root of their problems. In some ways it's inevitable that if your children aren't eating properly, you are going to worry about them. But children will often pick up on your anxiety, and it will make them feel anxious too.

Zora's twins had been born two months prematurely. They were in intensive care, and it was touch and go as to whether they would survive. Zora was unable to breastfeed them, and had found the bonding process difficult. 'It was really stressful. I remember just sitting there, crying, trying to express and hardly getting anything,' she recalled. Stress had dented her confidence as a mum, and three years later she was still feeling that she couldn't feed her daughters properly.

The twins would also get anxious very easily and react to Zora's stress. Zora had never previously made this connection. 'I'd never thought that the reason I was stressed out about them not eating was because I couldn't feed them when they were tiny,' she said. 'It was obvious, if you think about it.'

Anxiety is called the fight/flight syndrome, and is a primitive, in-built response to dealing with threat. This means that when we feel threatened and become anxious we either fight the source of our anxiety or run away from it. This happened with Zora at mealtimes, when she either became frustrated and battled with her children (the fight response) or withdrew and allowed the girls to take control of their eating (the flight response). In a mirror image of her behaviour, the girls would also show a fight or flight response, either by battling with her or not eating, thus maintaining a vicious cycle.

Attitudes and habits formed during the early years can help establish good habits for life. If we as parents want to encourage healthy eating patterns, we need to look at the messages our children get about food and feeding from our behaviour towards them at mealtimes. The best way to help your children be relaxed and happy about eating is to behave in a similar way yourself.

Understandably, you may find it hard to relax about your child's eating, especially if you are worried that he or she may not be eating enough, or a wide enough range of food. Even though you know that your behaviour at mealtimes may have contributed towards the development of the problems, you may find it hard to break an anxious cycle of behaviour with your child because you are worried about his or her health. The first thing to do is to reassure yourself that your child is healthy. Some ways of doing this are outlined below.

What is normal?

By 15 months old, most children have developed enough fine motor skills to feed themselves without help, if allowed to do so. All children are individuals, and their appetites will vary. If you have more than one child, you will see the differences between them.

There are two key questions to ask about any child with feeding difficulties:

1 Is he consuming enough calories to be a good weight for his height?

2 Is he eating a good range of foods and getting a healthy balance in his diet?

Your health visitor or GP can help you address your anxieties by weighing and measuring your child. They will plot the results on a growth chart, which is a reliable way to tell if your child's diet is meeting her bodily needs: you will be told which percentile your child is on for weight and height. This means that if your child were to be lined up with 99 other children from the lightest to the heaviest, her position in the line would reflect how she is doing. If she is on the 50th percentile, she would be in the middle of the line-up and regarded as average; anything above that percentile is above average, and less than 50 is below average.

Since we all come in a variety of sizes, it is not just where on the scale your child fits that matters, but that she continues along broadly the same lines. A child who is on the 50th percentile for his first two years of life is likely to stay roughly along that line, but if he suddenly dropped to the 25th for weight while his height stayed on the 50th, you might then want to look at the weight loss. Children grow in spurts, but if their weight has suddenly dropped down the scale, they may not be consuming enough calories for their size.

If your child is far below, or above, average, your health visitor, GP or a dietitian can advise about healthy feeding and the appropriate calorie intake.

Mealtime battles
Yssis

Yvette Edwards was extremely worried that her three-year-old daughter Yssis wasn't eating. Yssis had been hospitalized twice in the preceding two years with a gastric bug and pneumonia. On both occasions she had lost a lot of weight, and Yvette was terrified of this recurring. She was also very concerned that Yssis wasn't growing. She had been back and forth to the doctor several times, but did not feel reassured. Yvette had previously raised two other children, who were healthy eaters, so she found her problems with her third child surprising and baffling.

Yvette's anxiety had translated into the fight part of the fight/flight response, and her desire to make Yssis eat ended up in a stand-off at every meal. Mealtimes had become a battle of wills. 'It's like a chore for her and a chore for me. She knows what to expect and I know what to expect, and it's day in, day out,' Yvette said. Meals could drag on for anything up to two hours. 'There have been times when I've actually gone to sleep feeding her because she's taken so long,' Yvette admitted.

Yvette was worried that Yssis had a really entrenched eating disorder. However, filming revealed that she actually did eat, although not always at mealtimes. What her mother didn't see was that when her back was turned Yssis was climbing up on the kitchen units to steal sweets, and was pestering her older brother and sister to give her biscuits and milkshakes, even in the middle of the night.

When Yvette saw her behaviour tape she realized that she was setting up every mealtime as a battle with Yssis, and in doing so was making it less likely that her child would eat. Her frustration created a vicious cycle: the more she nagged her to eat, the less Ysiss felt like it; the less Yssis ate, the more stressed and anxious Yvette became. In fact, with two older children to care for, as well as Ysiss and newborn baby Osaru, Yvette was already very stressed. 'Sometimes I think I'm just tired of dealing with her,' she realized. 'I just want a break.'

Breaking the cycle

If you take the stress out of mealtimes, they are likely to be much more enjoyable for your children, which will give them a more positive message about food and eating. Here are five steps that will help you to achieve this.

1 Calm down

The most important thing you can do if you're locked into a pattern of anxious behaviour is to try to break the cycle. Yvette was asked to change her behaviour with Yssis at mealtimes. She was no longer to chivvy her daughter in any way: no threats, no cross words and no nagging.

As she played up at mealtimes, Yssis was still strapped into a high chair at the age of three, and often ate alone in the kitchen, long after the other children had left. It was suggested that Yvette get rid of any negative associations by creating a new eating space in the front room and allowing Yssis to sit on a chair. She also replaced her usual large bowl and spoon with some fun bowls and cutlery designed for a small child.

Yvette was coached through the earpiece at the first meal under the new system. First she read Yssis a story to relax her before bringing in the food. As soon as food was mentioned, however, Yssis began to get tense, so Yvette was asked to engage her in laying the table with her fun new cutlery as a way of distracting her. It was also suggested that Yvette give Yssis a smaller portion than she usually did, as a large portion can sometimes seem daunting to a small child.

During the meal Yvette had to refrain from making any negative comments, or giving any commands, such as 'Eat up' or 'Sit up properly'. Instead, she was asked to give lots of praise for eating and to make a running commentary on what Yssis was doing: 'Oh look, you managed to get a really big piece of pasta.' Yssis immediately tucked into her food, and when she seemed to be stopping, Yvette was asked to reposition her bowl in front of her gently, without comment. Without any reminders to eat, Ysiss happily returned to her food in between chatting. When she stopped it was suggested that Yvette say, 'Have you had enough?' instead of the more challenging, 'Have you finished?'

'It was a bit hard in some places, and I had to bite my lip when she was messing about and fidgeting,' said Yvette afterwards. But compared to a previous mealtime, she rated her stress at two points out of a possible 10. Over the next few weeks Yvette had to rate her anxiety levels out of 10 at every meal. The more relaxed she was, the more her anxiety levels dropped.

When baby Osaru began to disrupt meals with his demands, Yvette's stress levels rose and she began to nag Yssis again. To try to distract herself and Yssis from the stress, Yvette was asked to start chatting to Yssis and see how she would behave better. What Yvette was learning was that the way Yssis behaved at meals was directly related to her own stress levels.

A visit to a dietitian confirmed that Yssis was a normal weight for her height, which also helped Yvette to relax. The dietitian suggested that two tablespoonfuls of each type of food was plenty for her. 'Smaller portions work well,' Yvette realized. 'If she wants more, she'll ask for it.' After a few weeks things were much improved. 'I still get stressed out,' said Yvette, 'but not as much as I did before.' There was a bonus too: now that Yssis was eating far better during the day, she stopped waking her sister during the night and asking her to make milkshakes.

2 Have fun with food

Food shouldn't be a serious business. A great way of breaking a negative pattern is to surprise your child with a new approach. You can play games while shopping for food, or try cooking together, when you can encourage your child to dip her fingers into various things and taste different flavours.

Yssis and Yvette went on a picnic together, which helped them build a more positive relationship. The picnic allowed Yssis to play with food and make more of a mess than she would normally be able to. Yvette put a blob of jam on her daughter's nose, which Yssis loved, and asked her to play 'name the fruit'. She let Yssis make her own messy sandwich, which Yvette then had to taste.

Zora Lunniss's anxiety over food meant that twins Elodie and Asha hadn't been taught to enjoy fruit and vegetables. When we are anxious about something we tend to avoid it, and soon become unable to face it at all; this is called a phobia. Asha and Elodie were phobic about fruit and vegetables, and had learnt to reject them automatically by throwing them off their plates. To help them feel less anxious, they were made to face these foods while having fun.

Both girls were presented with a range of fruit and vegetables and asked simply to play with them. They made funny teeth out of carrot

---

HOW TO AVOID FUSSINESS

Many young children are fussy and might eat only a few self-selected foods. In this case, remember the following:

○ Don't fuss. When a parent nags, the child is less likely to try new foods.

○ Finicky food habits are often temporary, and will disappear if not reinforced by your negative behaviour or unnecessary rules.

○ Do not use food to bribe or punish.

○ If a food is rejected, do not make a big deal of it, as this could make your child more determined to refuse it next time it is offered.

○ Present new foods at the beginning of the meal when your child is really hungry. Serving a small amount of a new food alongside a favourite food may help your child to accept it.

○ Keep food simple. Most children enjoy the true flavour of foods without sauces, syrups, herbs or spices.

sticks, cut open apples to see where the juice came from, and mashed up strawberries and blueberries in yoghurt. Despite their initial resistance even to touch these foods, the girls were soon experiencing colour, taste and textures in a non-threatening way, and thus feeling less anxious. They were learning that fruit and vegetables could be a positive experience – the first step on the road towards eating them.

3 Use distraction and motivation

Zora had got so used to negative interactions at mealtimes that she had to learn to make meals more fun. She used distraction to engage the girls in a more playful way: 'Oh look, Elodie, is that a very naughty carrot? Do you want to break it?' she asked. Elodie was immediately intrigued.

Zora also used stickers and stories to help motivate the girls. The first sticker they got was for sitting on their chairs nicely. Zora worried that the girls would become more interested in the stickers than the food, but this did not matter as they were enjoying themselves. The girls were praised for beginning to eat, and given another sticker as motivation for having a few more mouthfuls. In the meantime, Zora distracted them with a story about Mr Carrot and his carrot bed, house and curtains.

When Elodie left the table and started having a tantrum, Zora had to use the opposite approach to usual. Normally she would have given all her attention to the twin having the tantrum. This time she gave attention and another sticker to Asha, who was still sitting and eating. This strategy worked, as Elodie wanted a sticker too; she came back to the table and ate a bit more. 'I'm having to rethink everything I've done and start all over again,' admitted Zora. 'I feel more determined to get them eating more varied food. It's going to be a gradual process, but that's the only way to deal with it.'

4 Increase the range of foods

If you're worried that your child won't eat a wide range of foods, and, in particular, won't eat fruit and veg, it's important to keep offering them nonetheless. It's easy to fall into a negative pattern of thinking,

'She won't eat that,' which means you are less likely to offer your child that food again.

In fact, it's instinctive for a toddler to reject a new food, and you may need to offer it up to 20 times before a child accepts it. This does not mean giving your child sprouts at every meal and then getting upset when he doesn't eat them. Just put a little bit of a new food on his plate every so often, and ignore any comments, such as 'Yuck'. If he doesn't touch it, simply remove the plate at the end of the meal without comment. If and when he does try a new food, give him lots of praise for doing so. If he tries it and really doesn't like it, try offering it again a few weeks later, but, as before, don't make a fuss if he doesn't want to eat it. You should try to introduce only one new food at a time, and only in a small quantity. Remember to keep calm and positive; use games and creative ways to encourage your child to try a new food.

5 Take control

Both Zora and Yvette had to deal with the issue of who was in control at mealtimes. Zora needed to take back the control that she had given her twins by being firm and clear about how and when they ate, while being more fun and encouraging. Yvette needed to give Yssis more control over eating by letting her sit on a chair and feed herself at her own pace, rather than being nagged and fed by her mother.

When you think about your children and mealtimes, be realistic about who controls the various aspects of their eating. With younger children, you have control over what and when they eat. But as soon as your child can hold food and put it into her mouth, you should encourage self-feeding and allow her to take control of this, while you continue to control her diet and mealtimes. Do not worry about mess as your child learns to feed herself, and do not wipe her continually. This will only make the situation fraught and start off a negative cycle. Children need to make a mess to learn; your anxieties about this shouldn't become theirs.

HOW TO MAKE MEALTIMES A PLEASANT EXPERIENCE

Mealtimes are a good opportunity for families to spend time together and talk, so try to eat at least some meals together if you can. Good eating habits learnt in childhood can develop into healthy habits for life.

Food and feeding

○ Involving your children in making meals will increase their interest in new or unfamiliar foods.

○ Include at least one of your child's preferred foods in a meal.

○ Offer foods with a variety of colours and textures to appeal to your child's senses and to increase the number of foods he will accept.

○ Include finger foods; children may try a new food if it is prepared attractively, such as cut into interesting shapes.

○ Serve child-size portions, 1–2 tablespoonfuls of each type of food to start with. You can always offer more, but do not pile up the plate.

○ Let children feed themselves as much as possible and decide how much they want to eat. Allow very young children to touch their food and eat with their fingers, even if this means mess.

○ Remain calm if your child leaves part of an entire meal untouched.

○ Never try to force your child to eat something he doesn't want.

○ If your child hasn't eaten any of her main meal, do not offer pudding.

Behaviour – yours and your child's

○ Try to work around a consistent feeding schedule, but be flexible if your child becomes too tired or hungry.

○ Make sure your child is not too excited from play or too tired to eat.

○ Have a routine, such as washing hands, to get ready to eat.

○ A comfortable eating environment is important. Use chairs, plates and cutlery suitable for your child's age. Seat your child straight up and facing forward in her chair.

○ Sit with your child while he eats, or stay close by. Don't leave younger children unattended.

○ Do not overwipe children; once at the end of a meal is enough.

Bad behaviour at mealtimes

Not all parents have difficulty getting their children to eat, but some find setting clear boundaries around bad behaviour at mealtimes just as problematic as at other times. Parents can help reinforce good meal-time behaviour by applying the same principles as to other kinds of behaviour.

Herbie, Miles and Ella

Nigel and Bianca Price were fed up with their three children, Miles, Herbie and Ella (seven, five and three respectively), causing mealtime chaos, which often triggered rows between them. 'I'd love the children just to be able to sit there and eat their dinner without belching, fighting and dropping stuff,' said Nigel. 'It's a chimps' tea party every time. I'd love it to be more civilized.'

Nigel and Bianca were asked to agree between them the behaviour that they expected. They then had to draw up a clear list of rules for mealtimes, and implement a reward system for following them:

O As the children were always charging off in the middle of meals, Nigel and Bianca decided that they wanted them to stay sitting at the table until the end. They then had to ask to get down.

O Nigel would become irritated by Bianca having to feed Herbie to get him to finish his food, so they made eating unaided another rule.

O To make this easier, they also agreed that they would put less food on the children's plates.

O They decided they would not let the children have pudding if they didn't eat what they were asked to.

They drew up a simple sticker chart (see opposite) that gave the children a clear message on the behaviour they wanted.

Using the earpiece, Nigel and Bianca were talked through manag-ing the children's mealtime behaviour and picking up on the early warning signs that might lead it to deteriorate. First they had to keep chatting to the children to distract them from lapsing into silliness. When Ella got down from the table and began to roll on the floor she was clearly told that she would not get her sticker if she was not back

MEALTIME BEHAVIOUR CHART (kept for the Price children)

	Miles	Herbie	Ella
Sitting nicely	★	★	★
Using knife and fork	★	★	★
Feeding yourself	★	★	★
Eating all Mum and Dad say	★	★	★
Asking to leave table	★	★	★

at the table by the time Bianca counted to three. This worked, but soon another child was threatening to play up. Herbie started to get upset while Miles was dominating the conversation; he had to be distracted and engaged in talking about something that interested him.

At the end of the meal the children were quickly given their stickers so that they would associate them with their good behaviour. They were rewarded with chocolate ice creams for pudding, and Nigel was happy. 'I really enjoyed that meal,' he said. 'It's great not to have that hassle.'

Ayla

Three-year-old Ayla Huseyin was using her eating behaviour to control and dominate her parents by demanding different foods and having long, loud tantrums. Her mother Alev would panic, and respond by opening new packets of food. When Ayla would eat her toast only if cut into a specific shape, her mother spent ages drawing shapes on a piece of paper to try to understand what she wanted. Alev and Ayla would end up screaming at each other, while 18-month-old Esin would be getting no attention for sitting in her high chair and eating quietly.

Watching their behaviour tape, Ayla's parents Alev and Somer soon realized that they were responsible for Ayla's behaviour because they had given her complete control of mealtimes. They were reinforcing

Ayla's refusal to eat by offering her a variety of alternatives, and giving all their attention to her for not eating, while ignoring the child who was eating.

In order to regain control, Alev and Somer adopted the following tactics:

○ They gave Ayla her meal and ignored her if she started a tantrum or refused to eat.

○ They would lavish Esin with praise for eating nicely.

○ If Ayla started eating, Alev and Somer would praise her for being a good girl.

○ If Ayla refused her food, they would try to distract her with a song or a story.

○ If Ayla started to make demands, they would calmly but firmly say no.

○ If Ayla started to have another tantrum, they would ignore her.

○ If Ayla continued the tantrum and her parents could feel things were escalating, they would ask her to stop – once nicely, then once firmly.

○ If Ayla did stop and came to the table, she would get lots of praise.

○ If she still didn't stop, she would be put into time out (see page 71). Afterwards her parents were to carry on as normal.

Alev and Somer quickly found that presenting Ayla with clear choices, and ignoring the behaviour they didn't want, greatly diminished her tantrums. Ayla had a tantrum when she wasn't allowed cream cakes for breakfast, but this was ignored too. 'I don't want to make a meal of what she's doing,' Somer said when Ayla was having a tantrum, 'so I'll ignore her – and it works.' Alev was reassured that life at home was becoming far less stressful. 'I feel as if they know that Mummy and Daddy are the people who have the final say, which makes such a world of difference in the household,' she said.

Rio, Carlo and India

Space was tight for Tracy Ellmore: she had a small kitchen and front room, and no table and chairs, so her three-year-old triplets Rio, Carlo and India had simply never learnt to sit at a table. Meals were eaten sitting on the floor in the front room, and chaos ruled, with the children spinning their plates, doing handstands in the middle of dinner and tipping food down the sofa. 'You've got to try and get them to eat their dinner first of all, then you've got to try to get them to eat it without tipping it everywhere; make them sit down; then try and clean up after them, while stopping them from doing other stuff,' grumbled their mother.

Tracy had not set clear limits for the triplets in terms of what she expected from their behaviour. The first step was for her to get a table and chairs. Next, she had to sit the triplets down, praise them for sitting nicely, and set consequences if they did not behave as she wanted them to.

At first, Tracy wasn't at all confident that she could get the triplets to behave well at table. She was taught to implement a clear series of consequences, which involved making the children stand in the corner, where she could see them, then go into time out if they did not do as they were asked. The time out system was a shock to them, but they learnt to

---

TIPS FOR GOOD BEHAVIOUR AT MEALTIMES
○ Meals should be eaten in a high chair or at a table and without the TV on. The atmosphere should be fun and focused on enjoying the meal rather than a programme.
○ Expect and tolerate child-like table manners while gently establishing your mealtime rules.
○ Show children your own good table manners; they will learn from your example.
○ Give lots of attention and praise for sitting nicely and eating up.
○ Keep children engaged with chat.
○ Ignore the behaviour you don't like, such as tantrums.
○ Use distraction techniques if behaviour starts to deteriorate.
○ Set clear boundaries around the behaviour you would like to see.
○ Use consequences, such as no pudding, if children behave badly.
○ Motivate your children by using a sticker chart focused on specific behaviour you would like to see.

sit and eat at the table very quickly. 'They're a lot calmer now,' said Tracy. 'I think they understand that if they sit down and eat all their lunch nicely, they'll get a yoghurt. If they mess around, they won't get one.'

Other mealtime issues

Joint approach

Make sure that you and anyone else involved in feeding your child uses the same clear and consistent approach. If children get a confused message because their treatment at mealtimes varies according to the person they are with, their behaviour will get worse. Somer Huseyin let Ayla have an ice cream in a restaurant after she had not eaten her lunch and her mother had told her she would get no pudding. He was both undermining his wife's authority and giving his daughter a mixed message about how she could behave, making it more likely that she would play up again and expect an ice cream.

Siblings

If you are dealing with more than one child, make sure that all the children are given the same message about food and eating. If they are all problematic, a sticker chart, such as the one used with the Price children (see page 119), could be effective, as the spirit of competition will motivate them to behave well.

Obesity

The incidence of obesity among children is rising at an alarming rate, and it's clear that being overweight can have adverse physical, social and emotional consequences. When thinking about your children's diet and feeding habits, also consider how much exercise they have: their appetites will be better if they are outside running around rather than inside on the sofa watching TV. It's also best not to use food as treats because you will be conditioning your children to have an unhealthy relationship with it. They may come to associate food with comfort when they are feeling down, and begin to turn to food rather than other types of support, which could lead to weight gain.

Breastfeeding

Many mothers wean their babies off the breast during the first year, but if you continue longer, you may need to find a way of making it clear to your child when you want it to stop.

Four-year-old Nicola Georgiou had developed domineering and controlling behaviour around this aspect of feeding. She was the youngest of three children, and a much-wanted girl, born six years after the second of her two brothers. Christina had enjoyed breastfeeding Nicola, but decided to wean her off at the age of two. Nicola, however, was insistent that she wanted to continue.

At the age of four, Nicola was still breastfeeding. She would latch on to her mother's breast whenever they were alone and her mother was on the phone. Christina would become so desperate that she would even phone her husband Dee at work to get him to tell Nicola to stop.

A lack of clarity about breastfeeding had given Nicola a confused message about her behaviour. Both Dee and Christina were unwittingly reinforcing the behaviour by arguing with her about stopping while still allowing her to do it. The breast was called 'titty' and had a real presence within the whole family. When Nicola was feeding, Christina would initially say no, but then give in to her and even cuddle her, giving a mixed message about what she expected. Christina was only able to show Nicola that she really meant no by putting her foot down and imposing consequences if Nicola was aggressive.

If you are having trouble weaning your child off the breast, remember to:

❍ Remain calm.
❍ Wean her off gradually.
❍ Distract her if she becomes upset.
❍ Stick to what you want to achieve.

POINTS TO REMEMBER

○ Children can use their behaviour at mealtimes to control and manipulate their parents by:

- Refusing to eat.
- Not eating enough.
- Being very fussy and demanding about what they eat.
- Behaving badly at table.

○ Your behaviour will be central to your child's poor eating and mealtime habits. Monitor the problem by keeping a simple diary for a minimum of one week. Does your child have a problem with feeding, or is he behaving badly? Try to decide which is the main problem before you take action.

○ What does the behaviour mean?

- Is your child getting a varied enough diet?
- Is he refusing to eat certain foods?
- Are you locked in a battle of wills with your child at mealtimes?
- Have you given your child control of his eating habits?
- Are you giving most attention to your child's bad behaviour at mealtimes and thus reinforcing the problem?

○ Anxiety is a primitive response to dealing with threat. If your child's eating makes you anxious, recognize how your anxiety affects:

- The way you respond to your child (either fight him or withdraw and give in).
- His behaviour at mealtimes (to fight you or withdraw and eat very little).

○ Think about your child's behaviour compared to what is 'normal'.

- By 15 months old most children have developed enough fine motor skills to feed themselves without help, if allowed to do so. Let them learn.
- All children are individuals, and their appetites will vary. If you

have more than one child, you will see the differences among them.

● Is your child consuming enough calories to be a good weight for her height?

● Is your child eating a good range of foods and having a healthy balance in his diet?

❍ Taking the stress out of mealtimes will make them much happier occasions, and will give your child a more positive message about food. You can do this by:

● Calming down.

● Having fun with food.

● Using distraction and motivation.

● Slowly and creatively increasing the range of foods in your child's diet.

❍ Think about who has the control when your child is eating. Let children control feeding themselves as much as they can, and tolerate any mess they make. Retain control over their mealtimes by helping them learn to enjoy a healthy and balanced diet.

❍ If your child is fussy, recognize that this is normal and that you might need to introduce a new food up to 20 times before she accepts it. If she rejects it, ignore her and offer it another time. If a tiny bit goes into her mouth, give her lots of praise. Stay calm, relaxed and optimistic.

❍ If your child behaves badly at mealtimes, start setting clear boundaries around his behaviour. Apply the same principles as to other kinds of behaviour – by ignoring what you don't want and praising what you do. You can use other behavioural techniques, such as sticker charts and time out to give impact to new rules.

❍ Food is essential to life, and our relationship with it should be healthy and fun. Help your children learn good eating habits by thinking about how your behaviour affects theirs. If you want your child to eat up, you must relax and take the stress out of mealtimes.

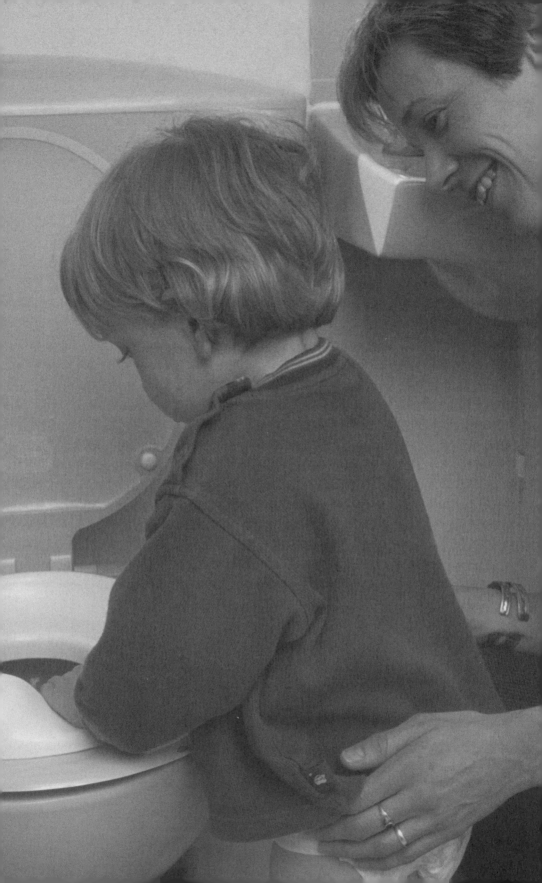

chapter seven

Going potty

MANY PARENTS FIND GETTING THEIR CHILDREN OUT OF NAPPIES AND ENSURING THAT they stay clean and dry a stressful business. Parents of toddlers are often fiercely competitive over what age potty training is achieved, and compare their child's performance to that of other children. Friends and relatives can add to the pressure, with their own claims of training their children at a very young age.

For some parents potty training goes smoothly, and once trained, their child stays that way. But it can be struggle for many others, and there are also those children who lapse into regular accidents after they have been trained. Getting these children back on track can become a real problem.

There are three main areas of toilet training:

1 Dry by day
2 Dry by night
3 Bowel control

What is normal?

Most children develop the necessary physical and cognitive skills to start toilet training between 18 and 24 months old, and can begin to hold urine for short periods. Girls are usually quicker to learn bladder and bowel control than boys, but each child is an individual, and you may see differences even within families of same-sex children.

If your child is already doing some of the following, he or she might be ready to start potty training:

❍ Walking and sitting down.

❍ Following simple instructions.

❍ Taking an interest in and mimicking you or her siblings using the toilet.

❍ Wanting to be independent, such as trying to dress himself.

❍ Able to pull pants up or down unaided.

❍ Using words such as 'poo' and 'wee', especially as she is doing them.

❍ Having dry periods of 3–4 hours (indicating that bladder muscles are developing).

❍ Indicating that she dislikes being in a dirty nappy.

❍ Grunting or showing in other physical ways that he is doing a poo.

You shouldn't worry about your child having accidents while learning; these may occur for up to six months after potty training. As a broad rule – and of course there are exceptions – many children are dry during the day by the age of two, and nearly all will be dry by three. Most do not soil themselves beyond the age of three, and are dry at night by the age of three and a half. If your child is still having problems beyond this age, or if his training is affected by constipation or diarrhoea, you should consult your GP or health visitor.

While your child is potty training, and especially in the early months after training, you need to plan outings and activities carefully. You will need to remind your child to use the toilet regularly, and you should always carry a change of clothes, plastic bags and wipes. Being in a public place or at a social occasion with a child who has wet or soiled himself is not pleasant, but is best dealt with by changing him quickly and without fuss. Don't worry what other people are thinking.

When there are problems

Training your child to use the toilet is similar to teaching her a healthy sleep pattern or good table manners. You need to be clear about what you want in a relaxed way, using incentives and praise to motivate her, while ignoring any mistakes. If your child has trouble using the toilet,

TIPS FOR SUCCESSFUL POTTY TRAINING

○ Do not start your child too early. Often children can indicate when they are able to hold their urine or need to pass a motion.

○ Do not compare your child to others and get anxious that he or she is taking longer. All children are different and are ready to learn at different times and at different rates.

○ Be relaxed and positive about training. Take it at your child's pace.

○ If possible, train in the summer, when potties can go in the garden and accidents can be more easily tolerated.

○ Every time your child successfully uses his potty or the toilet praise him as much as you can.

○ Be creative in making potty time fun; sing and read stories.

○ Use incentives to encourage your child: cuddles and a big family cheer around the potty work wonders for your child's learning. With children of three and over you can use sticker charts.

○ Do not be negative about smell if your child wants to proudly show you what she has done.

○ Recognize that having accidents is part of learning to stay clean and dry, so do not criticize or punish your child.

○ Be matter of fact about accidents and give them very little attention.

○ If you are anxious about your child toilet training, he will be too. This will have a negative impact on his learning.

○ Learning to use the toilet should not be tense, fraught or hostile. Encourage rather than nag; praise rather than chastise.

you need to think about how you are reacting to the problem and how that might be affecting the situation.

If you are struggling with early training, think carefully about the message you are giving your child. Are you tense? Do you feel and appear upset if he has an accident? Do you find it hard to tolerate mess or smell, and therefore make it a big deal? The more negative your response to your child's attempts to train, the more likely you are to have a negative outcome.

SAMPLE TOILET-TRAINING DIARY

1 Day/Date/ Time	2 Where are you? What's happening?	3 What did your child do?	4 What did you do?	5 Outcome

Using a diary

If you feel that you are in a negative cycle with your child over using the toilet, you will need to monitor what is happening over several days and consider how your responses may be affecting her. Keeping a diary (see above) is a good way of doing this.

Each column will give you important information about your child's problem:

1   Is there a time of day when your child is most likely to have accidents? If so, is there anything this could be linked to?

2   Are there particular triggers to her wetting or soiling? Is it when she is distracted, excited or wanting attention?

3   When and how did the accident occur? Did he hide? Did he do it blatantly in front of you? Did he talk about it?

4   How did you respond? Were you negative, tense, hostile? Did you shout, nag, criticize?

5   How did this affect her behaviour? Did she argue back or become upset?

The most important thing to understand from your diary is how you might have got into a negative interaction with your child around her toilet behaviour. If your behaviour is reinforcing the wetting or soiling by giving it a lot of attention, you will be making it more likely to keep happening. Also, if you are anxious about your child's behaviour, it will make her anxious and more likely to have accidents. The best example of this from *Little Angels* is the story of Nicola Georgiou.

From wet to dry

When we first met Nicola she was four years old and still wetting herself day and night. The youngest of three children, and the only girl, she was also having frequent tantrums and still breastfeeding from her mother Christina.

Nicola had been an easy child to potty train – dry by day at the age of two and a half, and dry by night at three. Just after she turned three, the family moved house and the children had to change schools. It was then that Nicola started to wet herself, initially at night, and then during the day as well. Christina was very concerned by this, as Nicola often smelt of urine, but would never admit to having wet herself. Whenever she wanted to wee, Nicola would run into the living room, hide behind the sofa and urinate on the carpet. 'During the day I think there's no excuse,' said Christina. 'She knows when she needs to go to the toilet. It's become a habit – she can't be bothered.'

Christina and her husband Dee were concerned that Nicola would have problems with other children at school if she did not stop wetting herself. At home there was frequent shouting between Nicola and her parents, and Christina was constantly washing wet sheets and clothes. Family outings were dominated by trying to prevent Nicola from wetting herself, and Dee, who ran a cab business, would not let Nicola sit in any of his vehicles in case she wet the seat. Nicola's wetting was causing problems for the whole family.

When viewing their behaviour tape, Dee and Christina had to recognize how their behaviour was contributing to the problem. Christina nagged her constantly about whether she wanted to do *bisha* (Greek Cypriot for 'wee'). When Nicola had wet herself the whole family would react, giving huge amounts of attention for it. Dee and Christina were also commenting every morning on Nicola's wet bed and asking her about why she was doing it. The whole situation was very tense.

So where were they going wrong?

○ They were giving Nicola lots of attention for wetting, and were thus reinforcing the behaviour, making it more likely to continue happening.

○ They were negative and critical towards Nicola when she wet herself, which made her behave in a secretive way, such as hiding and urinating behind the sofa.

○ They made Nicola's wetting very powerful in the family so that it disrupted family outings. This increased the likelihood of the behaviour recurring.

Christina and Dee first needed to accept that Nicola's lapse back into wetting from being dry was normal: children sometimes do this when they experience big changes in their life, such as a house move, changing schools, or the birth of a new sibling. Next they had to make a radical alteration in their approach to it.

Attention

As Nicola was getting far too much attention for her wetting, it was leaving her feeling embarrassed and anxious. Instead Christina and Dee were to:

○ Be calm and ignore her when she wet herself.

○ Be positive and encouraging when she stayed dry.

When Nicola wet herself Christina was told to say nothing as she quickly wiped and changed her. There was to be no conversation or eye contact, and thus Nicola would see that wetting got her no attention.

Tackling daytime wetting

To make Nicola feel positive about going to the toilet, she went shopping with her mother and bought a number of fun and pretty bathroom accessories: a seashore toilet seat, a pretty mermaid hand towel and a fun child's soap dispenser. All these were put into the downstairs toilet in a relaxed and calm way to make it 'Nicola's toilet'. There was no nagging that she must now use the toilet.

Incentives

A sticker chart was drawn up with Nicola to help motivate her and give her incentives to use the toilet:

○ Each day was split into three periods: morning, afternoon and evening.

○ For each use of the toilet Nicola would put a sticker on her chart, while Christina wrote the time underneath and gave her lots of praise.

○ If Nicola had an accident, Christina would say: 'Never mind, maybe next time,' and change her with no further attention and discussion.

○ For an accident a square would be drawn (not a cross, as on other types of sticker chart, because this is associated with doing something 'naughty') and the time noted underneath.

○ If Nicola was dry for an entire time period (i.e. all stickers and no squares), she got an extra big sticker, which meant that she got a little treat.

○ Each treat was given at the end of the time period, with lots of praise and an explanation why.

○ If she was dry all day, she got three small treats (not food).

By putting a sticker on the chart and making her feel really clever and special immediately after she did the behaviour that was required – the wee in the toilet – Christina soon taught Nicola what she wanted her to do. The chart also showed how Nicola was progressing day by day, and thus kept Christina's spirits up if there was an accident.

A relaxed and positive approach helped reduce Nicola's anxiety, and made her going to the toilet a normal part of the family routine. Nicola loved her new personalized toilet and quickly learnt to use it, which earned her lots of praise from her mother.

Tackling night wetting

Nicola was put back into trainer pants, which she chose, and this was introduced to her as a positive step rather than a failure. If the pants were wet in the morning, there was no attention or fuss. If she commented that they were wet, her parents very briefly said, 'Never mind,' and changed the subject. If they were dry in the morning, she got lots of praise. With no attention focused on the problem, Nicola soon relaxed. As she became more confident during the day, she quickly became dry at night too. 'Now she wakes up and says, "I haven't wet the bed today, Mum",' said Christina. 'And I say, "Well done!"'

POINTS TO REMEMBER
❍ Remain calm and relaxed.
❍ Don't nag your child to go to the toilet.
❍ Don't chastise or punish your child for accidents: just ignore them.
❍ Be realistic about when you start potty training; accept that your child is an individual and needs to go at her own pace.
❍ Praise all successes.
❍ Make the process fun – be creative.
❍ Use sticker charts to motivate children over three.
❍ Children who are dry and clean may lapse back into wetting or soiling after a change in their life. Don't make a big fuss about it.
❍ Always remember that your responses to your child's behaviour when learning to use the toilet will have the greatest effect on how successfully they learn.

chapter eight

The bigger picture

THROUGHOUT THIS BOOK WE'VE EXPLORED HOW TO MANAGE YOUR CHILD'S behaviour by looking at your own, and suggested simple strategies to help make your relationship happy and positive. But you may feel that there's still a piece of the puzzle missing in trying to work out what causes difficulties between you and your child.

Since we don't exist in a bubble, it's inevitable that the stresses of life are going to have an impact on how we feel about ourselves and on our relationships with our children. In trying to understand your problem, it often helps to look at the 'bigger picture'. It was also just as important for the *Little Angels* parents to recognize some of the other issues that had contributed to their problem as it was for them to look at the problem itself.

We are all unique, and our lives follow different paths. But looking back on the *Little Angels* families, all of whom made such positive changes to their children's behaviour, showed that several broad themes emerged to make up the 'bigger picture'. You may find it helpful to consider these.

Family problems
Your relationship with your partner
There's no doubt that children can put a huge amount of strain on a relationship, particularly if you are struggling with their behaviour. But

equally, if your relationship with your partner isn't going well, that can cause behaviour problems in children.

It's important that you both try to separate any problems in your relationship from your children as much as possible. Relationship break-down and disharmony are likely to confuse and upset children, which may be reflected in the way they behave. Also, parenting disagreements over responsibilities or discipline can enable children to manipulate the differences between you, and let them get their own way.

The parenting team

One problem we saw in a number of families was parents who weren't happy about the balance of roles and responsibilities between them. Matt Elson was trying to work from home, while his wife Mandie looked after their five children. Inevitably, he was constantly interrupted, and the lack of clear division in their roles was putting their relationship under strain. 'We've got to the stage where I've thrown the Yellow Pages at him open on the Relate page because I can't carry on like it any more,' said Mandie. Together they were helped to work out a new routine, which meant both felt much better supported as they went through each day.

Dee Georgiou thought he had no part to play in four-year-old Nicola's behaviour problems. As the family breadwinner, Dee thought that management of the children belonged with Christina's cooking and cleaning. He had to be helped to see that how he behaved was critical in solving Nicola's problems, particularly as he was undermining his wife by giving in easily to Nicola's demands. When Dee started to share the parenting with his wife, Nicola's behaviour began to improve.

Scott Wells also thought that his son Oliver's behaviour problems were his wife Vicki's responsibility. Scott wanted to be best mates with his son, and was unable to see that playing the kid with him made it very difficult for Vicki to parent Oliver with any consistency. All the discipline was left up to her, while Scott was taking all the good times. He was reluctant to impose boundaries, but accepted that he needed to restore balance to the family. 'I've realized that a lot of the time I haven't actually been doing the parenting,' he confessed.

Marital problems

When five-year-old Matthew Christie's parents Brian and Sarah contacted *Little Angels* they were getting back together after a period of separation. Matthew was difficult to manage, even at school, and his behaviour could be aggressive and unpredictable. His parents had to be helped to recognize that Brian's absence and the rows Matthew had witnessed had left him unsettled and anxious. 'There were times when I'd sit there and bawl my eyes out, and he'd come up and cuddle me and say, "Don't cry",' recalled Sarah. This had clearly had an effect on Matthew's behaviour.

Adam and Teresa Isherwood were shocked to realize that their six-year-old son Dominic did not have the behaviour problems that they thought he did. It was clear, however, that they had problems communicating as a couple, and there was tension in their relationship that they needed to recognize was not Dominic's fault. In fact, Dominic's 'bad' behaviour seemed to be one of the few things they could agree upon. By getting help with their marriage problems, they freed Dominic from his role as a receptacle for their bad feelings, and their relationship with him improved.

Remember:

❍ Children are good at exploiting splits between parents. Make sure you and your partner agree on strategies and have a consistent approach to your parenting responsibilities.

❍ Children may become distressed when they hear or witness marital discord. They are likely to express themselves with difficult behaviour because they lack the verbal skills to express how they are feeling.

❍ Do not use children as scapegoats for other problems within your relationship.

Single parenting

'It's so hard. People who've got two-parent families and one child find it difficult,' sighed single mother of triplets Tracy Ellmore. 'There's only me, and I've got three of them!' Nearly a quarter of all families in Great Britain, with nearly 3 million children between them, are headed by a lone parent. It's undoubtedly a tough and stressful job, particularly if you have financial difficulties or little support. But however hard it is, it shouldn't prevent you from adopting a positive approach to how your child behaves.

'I don't want to rock the boat with Keanu,' said Tamara Carrera, 'because I don't want people looking at me. Sometimes I think, "Can they tell I'm a single mum because I can't control him?"' To try to look as if she were in charge, Tamara would nag four-year-old Keanu whenever they were out together, unaware that her nagging was making his behaviour worse. Adopting a more positive approach helped her to stop feeling so critical of herself. 'I should be proud to have done as much as I have,' she realized. 'There's nothing to be ashamed of in bringing up a child on your own.'

Sometimes the break-up of a relationship can leave the remaining parent with residual anger. Lisa Williams realized that the bond she felt with four-year-old Kieran had been badly damaged by the break-up with his father. Lisa was confusing her negative feelings about her former partner with her feelings for Kieran; her negativity towards her child was having an impact on his behaviour. Lisa had lost sight of the fact that she was dealing with a four-year-old boy who needed her positive attention and affection. When he got this, Kieran began to behave better.

Many single parents struggle to find support that allows them to have some time on their own. Although Yvette Edwards had a partner, Michael, he did not live with her and her four children, and she realized that the stress in her relationship with three-year-old Yssis was partly down to the lack of breaks in her schedule. Yvette decided to ask Michael for more support so that she could get some time for herself. 'Having some time away makes me feel like me again, instead of being a mother 24/7,' she reflected. 'I was a person before I had children. It's like that bit of you gets taken away.'

Remember:

❍ Don't hold your children responsible for your bad feelings about other relationships.

○ If you are very stressed, it will affect your children. Try to find small amounts of time when you might be able to get some support and take breaks for yourself.

○ Even if you are parenting alone, you can still use a positive approach and consistent behaviour strategies, just as a two-parent family would do.

Step-parenting

'I don't like the things he tells me to do because he's not my daddy,' said eight-year-old Indianna Christoforou about her stepfather Lee. Indianna's mother Melissa had contacted *Little Angels* because she was concerned that her daughter's defiance, particularly towards Lee, was going to tear the family apart. 'How can we spend the rest of our lives together when he hates her?' she asked.

Approximately one in four marriages breaks up, and step-parents, as well as step- and half-siblings, are often created out of new relationships. Taking on someone else's children can come with all sorts of emotional baggage, and it can be hard to form a bond with them. Lee actually didn't hate Indianna, but felt that she had never accepted him, and now said he had 'given up trying'. Indianna was three when Lee joined the family and Melissa gave birth to his daughter, Violet. Lee was unaware that Indianna felt he paid her less attention than to his own daughter. But Melissa was shocked to discover that she too needed to bond more closely with Indianna, and that it was not just Lee who was responsible for Indianna's volatile behaviour.

Step-parents and stepchildren need time to develop their relationships and work out how to approach discipline. Lee had to find ways of getting back Indianna's respect before he could ask for any authority over her. By visiting an outdoor activity centre, where they did climbing and blindfold exercises to build the trust between them, Lee and Indianna began to bond. Lee encouraged Indianna by praising her more and listening to her when she was scared, and she responded to him. More importantly, he started to enjoy her company. 'I do think I'm more likely to do what he tells me because he's playing with me more, and that's fair,' said Indianna a few weeks later.

When Ivan Angell contacted *Little Angels* he was concerned that his nine-year-old stepdaughter Bethany had 'attitude'. The pair had had so many arguments that the bond that had previously existed between them had been lost. Although they shared many interests, Ivan now felt unsure about how to parent Bethany, and had pushed her away by being too strict. His attention was also mostly taken up with his younger daughter Emily's tantrums.

Ivan had to learn to have fun with Bethany again, by talking to her and giving her more praise and affection. His wife Sue also had to learn to deal with Emily's tantrums, freeing Ivan to develop a rapport with Bethany. Ivan felt defensive that Bethany wasn't his natural child, but realized while making the programme that he could love her in his own way, even if she wasn't his biological daughter. For the first time, he was able to ask her to call him Daddy.

Remember:
❍ A stepchild will need to be shown that he can trust you. If you work on developing special time and interests together, you can build the basis of a bond.
❍ If your child doesn't get on with your new partner, don't assume it's the child's fault.
❍ If you take on step-parenting a child, you and your new partner need to work out what role you will play in discipline and be consistent.
❍ You need to take into account what kind of emotional baggage a child may have from previous experiences and relationships.

Sibling rivalry
The chances are that if you have more than one child, they will fight. It is normal for siblings to fight among themselves, and is an important part of developing social skills to learn how to compromise and share. But fighting is a good way of getting parental attention, and there may be times when you need to step in.

Jo and Jason Barton's three boys never seemed to stop fighting. 'They squabble, they fight, there's always shouting, screaming, tears,' said Jo. As a busy working mother, Jo rushed around doing domestic chores when she was at home, and would leave the boys playing alone. Only when a fight broke out would she intervene. Jo and Jason had to recognize that they gave the boys most of their attention when they were behaving badly. In turn, the boys learnt that the best way to get their parents' attention was to fight.

Parents are often concerned about older children picking on younger ones. It's important before you jump to conclusions that you find out whether this is really the case, and ask yourself what their behaviour might be telling you. Nine-year-old Shelby Elson was fighting a lot with his six-year-old brother Tannar. His parents Matt and Mandie were concerned about his aggression. 'My mum says I'm the eldest and I should be setting an example,' said Shelby. But with three-year-old triplets in the family, Shelby felt that he got little attention, as well as the blame for anything that went wrong. 'If they ask me to stop shouting, I would tell them to stop shouting because they do it more than me,' he said.

Zoë Maynard was also concerned that six-year-old Sam was bullying his three-year-old brother Aaron, but she discovered that Sam's shouting and hitting often mirrored her own behaviour. Zoë started giving Sam calmer and more positive attention, and when it looked like a fight with Aaron was brewing she tried to separate the boys by distracting them with different activities. She also realized that Sam needed his own space to relax, and helped make a separate area in the bedroom he shared with Aaron.

Remember:
○ Don't set up sibling rivalry among your children by showing them that they can get your attention when they start fighting.
○ Don't automatically blame your older child or label her a bully.
○ Make sure you share your attention equally between all your children.
○ Don't take sides if you didn't see what happened.
○ Give children the message that their fighting won't get your attention by ignoring it, or try to divert them with distraction.
○ Set clear consequences, such as time out (see page 71) for any aggression that you do witness.

Other problems
After your child's birth

It may seem a long time since you gave birth to your child, but circumstances surrounding pregnancy, birth and the post-natal period can all have a lasting impact upon your relationship with him. If you had a very difficult birth, or if your baby was ill after birth, this may affect your feelings both about your child and yourself as a mother.

Some of the mothers who took part in *Little Angels* were surprised to learn that their problems had roots in the stress of the early life of their children. Zora Lunniss had never realized how her failure to bond with her premature twins and their early feeding difficulties had left her with feelings of anxiety and helplessness three years later. Similarly, Tracy Ellmore's three-month-premature triplets Rio, India and Carlo had very nearly died. Tracy had never completely recovered from her fear that something might happen to them. Three years later she was still afraid to let them out of her sight. In addition, Zora and Tracy both had to contend with a child's hearing problems caused by prematurity. This added to their confusion about how to manage difficult behaviour.

Five-year-old Jessica Butler had been born with mild cerebral palsy and a hole in her heart. Fears about her health had caused her parents Claire and Mick to treat her differently from her twin brother James. Over time Jessica had learnt to manipulate her parents' anxiety about her health because she knew that they would not crack down on her behaviour. Claire and Mick had to be shown that Jessica could in fact be treated exactly the same as her brother, and she became much calmer when firm boundaries were established.

Remember:

❍ It is common for parents of children with health problems or ongoing special needs to feel uncertain about how to deal firmly with difficult behaviour.

❍ Do not let your emotions or stress about your child conflict with your ability to set clear and calm boundaries.

❍ If your child had a difficult start in life, don't let your feelings about that time cloud your relationship with her now.

Post-natal depression

It is surprisingly common for mothers to suffer from post-natal depression. Several of the *Little Angels* mothers had suffered from it, and were brave and honest in talking about it. Post-natal depression can have an impact on how you bond with your baby, and can make it hard for you to enjoy and feel positive about him as he grows older. This, in turn, can lead to the development of behaviour problems. For this reason it's important that post-natal depression is recognized, and treated with either medication or therapy, or a combination of both.

Tamara Carrera had a very difficult pregnancy with four-year-old Keanu. Terrified of telling her family that she was pregnant and unmarried, she concealed her pregnancy until the eighth month. 'When I did have Keanu I couldn't bond with him because I felt, "Oh! I have a baby,"' she recalled. Her denial about the pregnancy had prevented her creating a bond with her child, and the guilt she later felt about this contributed to her confused and negative feelings about Keanu's bad behaviour.

Sam Norris had suffered a difficult pregnancy and traumatic emergency caesarian with her daughter Katie. Shortly after Katie's birth Sam's husband Tim had a serious motorbike accident. 'Katie and I were separated because I was at the hospital caring for Tim, and Katie was at his sister's,' Sam recalled. The impact of all this left Sam feeling depressed and finding it hard to bond with Katie. Three years on, Sam was helped to see how she was still linking Katie to a very traumatic time in her life and feeling negative about her, which contributed to Katie's problem behaviour. Sam needed to let go of these feelings to move on.

Teresa Isherwood had suffered from depression for many years, and also had post-natal depression after the birth of six-year-old Dominic, whom she now considered to be a problem child. She suffered from low self-esteem and a fear of socializing, which left her lonely and unsupported. Until she could get treatment for her depression, it would continue to affect her relationship with her son. 'Sometimes it makes me feel bad that my mother's being sad,' said Dominic. But as Teresa plucked up courage to make contact with other mothers and

POST-BABY BLUES

After having a baby, many women experience a short period of mild depression called the 'baby blues'. However, up to 10 per cent of new mothers go on to develop post-natal depression. It's important to seek help if you have some or all of the following symptoms:

- ○ Feeling unable to cope
- ○ Tense and irritable most or all of the time
- ○ Feeling guilty
- ○ Feeling sad
- ○ Crying a lot
- ○ Feeling anxious and worrying about your health and that of your baby; checking him often
- ○ Panic attacks
- ○ Feeling tired and without any energy
- ○ Difficulty concentrating or completing a simple task
- ○ Problems sleeping, despite being exhausted
- ○ Lack of appetite
- ○ No interest in sex

invite friends for tea, Dominic's view of his mother changed. 'It's a lot better because my mum isn't as angry as she was before,' he said. 'I feel really happy about it.'

Stress and anxiety

Stress and anxiety can affect our behaviour in a number of ways, and can also cause problems for our children. Children are barometers of mood, and their behaviour is often affected when they sense bad feelings and tension. Being relaxed and calm is an important skill of parenting, but it can be hard to learn and needs practice.

Alev and Somer Huseyin were both very stressed by their eldest daughter Ayla's behaviour problems, as well as the financial pressures of running their own dry-cleaning business. Things became worse when their third daughter Tulay was born. Alev needed help to recognize that her stress levels were contributing to Ayla's behaviour. Alev was taught to use stress-management techniques by finding a place within herself that she could retreat to mentally when the stresses of her day began to get to her. She visualized birds and trees, and would focus on that image to help her remain calm during Ayla's tantrums. She would also sing to herself and count backwards in threes from 100 in order not to allow angry thoughts and feelings to flood her mind and body. This helped her ignore the tantrum.

Children can also suffer from anxiety, and sometimes their behaviour problems can reflect their reaction to previous experiences. Kathy Cooper was concerned about her seven-year-old son Jay's aggression towards his five-year-old brother Owen. Jay had often witnessed Kathy being beaten up before she met her new partner, Jamie. This had left Jay feeling vulnerable and with little self-confidence. He would play aggressively and had problems with physical contact.

Kathy and Jamie were helped to recognize that Jay's anxiety was the primitive in-built fight or flight response to threat. He would often react to situations he found challenging, such as doing homework, either by becoming aggressive and confrontational (fight), or by crying and giving up (flight). To begin helping Jay with these difficulties, Kathy and Jamie had helped him confront a big fear of riding a bike without stabilizers. With encouragement, they got him past his aggression and tearful withdrawal and helped him to ride his bike unaided. This was a huge breakthrough, and the first vital step to Jay changing his negative view of himself from 'rubbish' to 'champion'.

Remember:
○ Our stress levels can have a direct effect on our children's behaviour.
○ It is normal at times to let children feel your stress, but if this happens a lot, you must find ways of preventing yourself taking it out on them.
○ Relaxation, creative visualization and distraction are all useful stress-management techniques to use during challenging times.
○ Your child may be anxious after difficult early experiences, so deal with her sensitively and build confidence slowly by helping her achieve realistic goals.

Life events

Upheavals and changes in life can have a huge effect on children. It is normal for children to show 'adjustment reactions' to change, and their behaviour may deteriorate. How you respond may make the behaviour worse. Reassure your child by remaining calm, clear and consistent in your parenting: as he gets used to the changes, his behaviour will settle.

Nicola Georgiou was three years old when her family moved house from London to Hertfordshire and she and her brothers started at new schools. Having previously been toilet trained, she started wetting herself again night and day. Her parents Dee and Christina were shocked at her regression, but they didn't realize that her wetting was a normal response to the life change. When they calmed down about the wetting and stopped giving it so much attention, it began to improve and soon stopped.

Somer and Alev Huseyin had just managed to get three-year-old Ayla into a better sleep and behaviour pattern when new baby Tulay arrived. All the progress they had made unravelled; they felt so despondent that they wanted to give up. However, after the initial exhaustion of Tulay's arrival, Alev and Somer calmly continued to use the techniques they had learnt and got Ayla's behaviour back on track.

Sometimes your life may not be turning out quite as you want, and this may affect your child too. Jane Soilleux was struggling to come to terms with the fact that her husband Barry didn't want any more children and that her third child, Emily, was going to be her last. This meant that Jane was still treating Emily like a baby at the age of three, giving her a bottle and not putting her to sleep in her own bed. As she was treated like a baby, Emily would often behave like one, with whinging and demanding behaviour. As soon as Jane came to terms with the fact that she needed to let Emily grow up, she showed her that there were new expectations of her behaviour.

Remember:
❍ It is normal for a child's behaviour to regress after a big life change, especially if things feel unsettled and unfamiliar. If you remain calm,

she will feel reassured and her behaviour will soon settle again.

○ The birth of a new baby can often trigger behaviour problems in siblings. This is a normal reaction and should be handled sensitively.

○ If, after a while, your child continues to show difficult behaviour, don't feel guilty about taking a firm line. He will feel less anxious and more settled if he knows where he stands.

○ Don't project your insecurities or other difficult feelings on to your child as it could affect her behaviour negatively.

POINTS TO REMEMBER

You may already have considered how your behaviour has an impact on that of your child. It is also important to reflect on other issues that could have contributed to your child's ongoing difficulties. Ask yourself:

○ What else was going on around the time that his problems began?

○ Were there any problems with or around the time of her birth?

○ Have there been any big life changes that could have affected his behaviour?

○ Has she been witness to any relationship problems or breakdown?

○ Has he lived in the midst of relationship tension and discord?

○ Are you holding her responsible for bad times or events in your life?

○ Are your stress levels impairing your ability to parent effectively?

○ Is your child anxious and either fighting you or withdrawing?

○ Are you anxious about other problems and either fighting with or withdrawing from your child?

○ Did post-natal depression affect your ability to bond with your child, and is it difficult to enjoy him?

○ Are you currently depressed and finding parenting a struggle?

○ Are you a single parent in need of support?

○ Are you in a step-family and need to address parenting and relationship issues?

○ Have your child's health difficulties or special needs left you with guilt or anxiety that make it hard to parent effectively?

While it is important not to overanalyse your child's behaviour problems, understanding a problem goes a long way to solving it. If you
have recognized yourself in any of the issues described in this book, it's
because you are a normal human being dealing with some of the many
complexities and challenges that life throws at all of us. With luck, this
will enable you to relax about your child and set his behaviour in con-
text to see that he is not a 'bad person'. As Sam Norris said of Katie,
'She's a better kid than we all thought. We just couldn't see it before.'

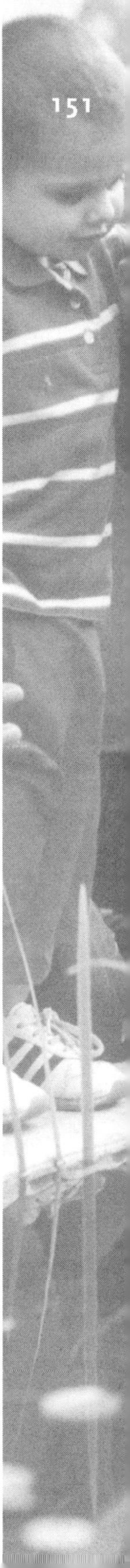

And finally...

THE QUESTION WE'RE OFTEN ASKED ABOUT *LITTLE ANGELS* IS, 'WHAT HAPPENED to the families after the cameras left?' We got the chance to find out just before Christmas 2004, when we decided to hold a *Little Angels* Christmas party. Every family who had taken part in the series was contacted. Sixteen of the 20 families we had originally filmed with came to the party, and we were delighted to see how well all the children behaved. Some families had had ups and downs, but all the parents remained very positive about the changes *Little Angels* had made to their relationship with their children. The problems they had resolved through making the programmes had not returned.

You might feel like you've had as much advice as you can stomach by now. But the fact that you've read this book means that, like those families, you care about your children and are trying to do your best for them. All of us juggle responsibilities in our lives, yet parenthood, the most difficult job of all, is the one there's no training for. Series such as *Little Angels*, and the suggestion that there might be a 'right' way of parenting, perhaps add to the sense of pressure.

Beyond all that advice, the most important aspect of being a parent comes from the instinctive pleasure of being with your children. Rather than becoming obsessed with trying to be a better parent, don't forget what your children can show you. Let them guide you with their uncomplicated and happy approach to life: the way they enjoy the moment, love to laugh and give hugs and kisses.

For your part, all you need to give your children are the following:
○ Love and praise so that they feel valued and special.
○ Cuddles and affection so that they know they are loved.
○ Routines and structure so that their life feels safe.
○ Clear boundaries so that they know where they stand.
○ Consistent rewards for doing well so that they build their self-confidence.
○ Clear consequences when they go wrong so that they can learn from their mistakes.

For their part, your children can, if you let them, enrich your life in a wonderful way. We hope that this book will have enabled you to feel confident and positive in the parenting of your children, and that above all it will help you to enjoy them as much as you possibly can. Good luck!

Acknowledgements

This book would not have been written without the courage and dedication of the parents and children who took part in the *Little Angels* series. We thank them all for rising to the challenge, working so hard and making such amazing changes.

Our thanks, too, to Stuart Murphy and his team at BBC3, who so passionately championed parenting on the channel. Also to Michael Mosley, John Lynch and Jill Fullerton-Smith, who were instrumental in getting the first series on air, and Reem Nouss, Camilla Lewis, Blue Ryan and Claire Beavis for their fantastic support over the last year. Huge thanks also to the entire *Little Angels* production team (listed overleaf), whose energy, talent and enthusiasm have made the series such a success and a pleasure to make.

We also would like to thank the other *Little Angels'* on-screen experts, Rachel Morris and Dr Stephen Briers, as well as Dr Wendy Casey, Jo Douglas and Dr Mark Berelowitz, for their off-screen consultation and support.

Emma Shackleton at BBC Worldwide, and our editor Trish Burgess, have kept us going with lots of positive praise while writing this book. We would also especially like to thank Samantha Richards for all her dedication and hard work.

As any mother knows, support networks are vital: Tanya would like to thank Sam Berlevy, Maria Papacostas and Kate Sprecher for being there, and Sacha thanks Jacqui Pusey. Above all, our love and thanks go to Bruce Byron and Duncan Ackery for keeping us going throughout; and big hugs to Lily and Jack Byron, and Evie, Tom and Teddy Ackery for reminding us why parenting is the best job ever.

The *Little Angels* team

Executive Producers: Jill Fullerton-Smith, Camilla Lewis, Reem Nouss
Series Producer (current Executive Producer): Sacha Baveystock
Line Producers: Clare Beavis, Blue Ryan
Directors: Alannah Richardson, Paul Olding, Alison Draper, Corinna Faith, Sophie Harris, Stephen Maud, Helen Seaman, Nicola Cook, Joanna Robinson, Fiona Inskip, Suzy Jaffe, Carrie Rose, Helen Scholes, Libby Turner, Rachel Scarrott, Miranda Michaelis
Assistant Producers: Kalita Corrigan, Melanie Heath, William Spiers, Nigel Shilton, Louise Wilson, Karina Griffin, Weini Tefsu, Nishi Bolakee, Farne Sinclair, Prim Bath, Sally Rose, Nathan Budd, Juliet Singer
Researchers: Helen Lambourne, Jenny Brown, Antonia Cavendish
Production Team: Sarah Ross McClean, Tom Berry, Cat Cubie, Anna McGill, Liz Collier, Shelley Raichura, Nicola Pinn, Seena Gosrani
On-screen experts: Dr Tanya Byron, Rachel Morris, Dr Stephen Briers

Picture credits

The following photographs are courtesy of Bubbles Photo Library for p. 6 and p. 22, photographer: Loisjoy Thurston; and the *Mother & Baby* Picture Library for p. 36, photographer: James Thompson; p. 58, photographer: Ian Hooton; p.78, photographer: Ian Hooton, p. 102, photographer: Paul Mitchell; p. 126, photographer: Jenny Woodcock; p. 136 photographer: Ian Hooton.

Further information

www.bbc.co.uk/parenting/
www.parentlineplus.org.uk 24-hour free helpline: 0808 800 2222
www.direct.gov.uk/Audiences/Parents
www.e-parents.org
www.oneparentfamilies.org.uk
www.workingfamilies.org.uk
www.parentcentre.gov.uk
www.raisingkids.co.uk

Index

relaxing 10, 40, 43, 47, 87, 109, 113, 125, 129, 147
response, parents' 13, 16, 21, 30, 41–50, 60, 65, 76, 101, 124, 129, 130 *see also* fight/flight
restaurant behaviour 61, 67–8
rewards 14, 26, 39, 45, 54, 56, 69, 118, 119
 withholding 66, 69, 76
routines 56
 bedtime 48–9, 79, 81–7 *passim*, 91, 92, 95, 100, 101
 mealtime 48–9, 117
rules 41–50, 53–6, 59, 61, 64, 66, 72–3, 76, 101, 118, 121
running away 70

scratching 61
screaming 10, 13, 16, 27, 29–30, 42, 67, 69, 93
self-doubts 25
self-esteem, low 10, 53, 145
self-fulfilling prophecy 27–8, 33
shopping 29, 45, 67, 70
 games with 113
shouting 8, 14, 15, 28, 30, 38, 39, 41, 42, 55, 61, 63, 64, 68, 108, 131, 143
shutting bedroom door 93–4
siblings 10, 97–8, 122, 142–3, 149
single parenting 25, 139–41, 149
sleep problems 9, 10, 24, 26, 79–101, 146
 deprivation 17, 21, 26, 79, 83, 91
 external props 86, 87, 101
 in front of TV 94
 in own bed 81, 92
 in parents' bed 10, 91, 94, 96–7
 requirements 84, 99, 100
smacking 30, 42, 71
snacks 105, 108
Soilleux, Barry 27, 83, 89–90, 148
 Emily 16, 27, 45, 70, 83, 89–90, 96, 148
 Jane 16, 27, 45, 83, 89–90, 148
step-parenting 28, 141–2, 149
stories, bedtime 86–7, 91, 92, 95
 mealtime 112, 115, 120
stress 12, 17, 28, 29, 42, 68, 109, 112–13, 125, 141, 144, 146–7, 149
sulking 16, 63
swearing 25–6, 61
sweets 14, 108, 111

table, behaviour at 103, 104
 manners 121
taking sides 143

tantrums 9–11, 13–17 *passim*, 21, 24, 26, 27, 40, 45, 63, 67, 68, 74, 76, 83, 86, 91, 108, 120, 121, 131, 142
tears 68 *see also* crying
teeth, cleaning 87
thanks 38, 65
threats 28, 30, 69, 109, 112
time out 58, 66, 71–6, 120, 121, 125, 143
 for parents 75
 points in brief 74
 when not to use 75
toilet behaviour 10, 54, 127–34
tolerance 66, 121
treats 14, 51, 53–5 *passim*, 95, 96, 133
 food as 54, 96, 122
triggers 11–13 *passim*, 20, 27, 35, 68, 130
TV 44, 46, 82, 83, 87, 88, 90, 92, 94, 100, 122

uncertainty 60
unlearning 15, 86, 89, 100
united front 56, 60–1
urinating 131–4

vegetables 105, 114–15
videos 17, 26, 86, 93
violence 17
voice, tone of 65
vomiting 40, 93, 99

waking, early 98
 in night 9, 80, 86, 91, 94, 96–8, 100, 101, 113
weaning 123
weight for height 110–11, 113, 125
 loss 111
Wells, Oliver and Vicki 8, 39, 43, 66, 70, 138
 Scott 138
wetting 131–4, 148
whinging 10, 27, 83, 148
Williams, Kieran and Lisa 16, 25–6, 46, 47, 73–4, 85, 87, 140
wiping hands/mouth 105, 116, 117
withdrawal 30
 gradual 88–90, 101